D1530788

"*The Savvy Grand........* has cleverly crafted personal stories that can easily be used as a daily devotional. This little gem is not only for grandmothers but for everyone who wants to impact the next generation."

—Ron Hall, grandfather of four and world-renowned speaker, champion of the homeless, and author of *Same Kind of Different as Me* and *What Kind of Difference Does it Make?*

"I've worn a lot of hats in my life, but none that meant more to me than that of 'grandma.' The number of young people who have addressed me by that title has now grown to nearly twenty (we have prolific children!), and I sometimes wonder if I'm all that 'savvy.' But *The Savvy Grandmother* has reminded me of just how savvy (and blessed!) I really am. If you're a grandma (or have one or even know one), you need to buy this book. In fact, buy several copies and give them as gifts. You will be blessing others as you do so, for we all need to rejoice in the privilege and honor of being a "savvy grandmother." Thank you, Marty!"

—Kathi Macias is a popular speaker and an award-winning author of more than thirty books, including her latest fiction release from New Hope Publishers, *People of the Book.*

"Wise, warm, and from the heart of one grandmother to another, *The Savvy Grandmother* makes a reader feel as if she's sharing coffee and great stories with a friend—a friend who makes you realize how important your role is in life. You'll learn, you'll laugh, you'll be inspired to revisit your past and share your own story of faith with your grandchildren. Using Marty's "savvy," you can not only make a difference now, but also leave future generations with a lasting, loving legacy.

—Marjorie Hodgson Parker, grandmother, author, newspaper columnist, and freelance writer, has written for magazines and children in "David and the Mighty Eighth," "Assault the Crippled Champion," and "Jellyfish Can't Swim." *Shaken to the Core (and Finding God's Strength)* is her new devotional for adults.

The Savvy Grandmother is for the grand generation of baby-boomer moms who are now grandmothers. Marty Norman encouraged those multi-tasking moms of "Generation G" to become savvy, life-managing grandmothers in her first book, and now in *Building a Legacy of Faith*, she's calling them to be savvy, life-giving, spiritual influencers of the next generation. Marty's voice as a writer—shaped by her own Christian life, a rich family life, and her experience as a counselor—is as personal and inviting on the page as it is in person. *The Savvy Grandmother* will speak to your heart, with stories and anecdotes to make every point poignant, and encouragement that is both comfortable and challenging. If you are a grandmother, your faith counts, and Marty will help you pass it on.

—Sally Clarkson, author of *The Mission of Motherhood, Seasons of a Mother's Heart, Dancing with My Father* and speaker for Whole Heart Ministries and Mom Heart Ministry.

The Savvy Grandmother sheds light on the power of legacy: the freedom we fight for, the traditions to which we hold fast; every tear, every smile, provides an offering of wisdom to our children's children.

—Wendy Saxton is the founder of The Medicine Place, an on-line ministry for women who seek healing from emotional wounds. She is the author of *The Jonah Chronicles: A Memoir of Hope for the Hopeless*.

the *Savvy* GRANDMOTHER

MARTY NORMAN

the *Savvy* GRANDMOTHER

BUILDING

A LEGACY

OF FAITH

TATE PUBLISHING
AND ENTERPRISES, LLC

Published by Tate Publishing & Enterprises, LLC
127 E. Trade Center Terrace | Mustang, Oklahoma 73064 USA
1.888.361.9473 | www.tatepublishing.com

Tate Publishing is committed to excellence in the publishing industry. The company reflects the philosophy established by the founders, based on Psalm 68:11,
"The Lord gave the word and great was the company of those who published it."

Book design copyright © 2012 by Tate Publishing, LLC. All rights reserved.
Cover design by Kenna Davis
Interior design by Christina Hicks

Published in the United States of America

ISBN: 978-1-61862-095-8
1. Religion / Christian Life / Family
2. Self-Help / Motivational & Inspirational
12.02.06

DEDICATION

This book is dedicated to the glory of God in thanksgiving for the influence and faith of my mother, Frances Morgan Gupton, my grandmothers, Frances VanZandt Morgan, Pauline Bolanz Seay, and Helen Wann Gupton, and my great-grandmother, Martha Binyon VanZandt. Their wisdom, love, and faith have been my inheritance, a gift passed down from generation to generation.

ACKNOWLEDGMENTS

First I want to thank God for the blessings that he has poured out on my life and my family. I pray that the words of my mouth and the mediations of my heart will bring honor and glory to his name.

Next I would like to thank the women in my family, who are my inspiration and role models. They have taught me to laugh, love, and live life to the fullest: Gangy, Shakey, Maman, Helen, Cecca, Auntie Mar, Rubye Faye, Aunt Sadie, Aunt Mary, Sally, Holly, and Blythe. Their lives and life experience have molded my own in ways that can't even be described.

I'd also like to thank those I've met in my travels: writers, grandmothers, career, single, and married women, who have opened their hearts and shared their stories of faith and salvation with me. Their witness has encouraged me to write this book, and their boldness has challenged me to be more than I ever dreamed I could be.

Next I would like to thank my prayer partners, those women who spend time on their knees before the Father on my behalf. Their support and words of encouragement have lifted me above and beyond my own ability and desire: Rhonda Albright, Suzan Cook, Becky Clute, Mary Ellen Davenport, Debbie Dittrich, Phyliss Dunn, Helen Epps, Christy Fonvielle, Tricia Gossett, Bobbie Harper, Suzanne Hearn, Nancy Komatsu, Rosalind Laird, Jeannie Ott, Debbie Petta, Candy Rehfeldt, Barbara Riley,

Sally Sledge, Carmyn Sparks,Meri Stanley, Janina Walker, and Belinda Whiddon.

Special thanks to my friends, Christy Fonvielle, Suzan Cook, Debbie Petta, and Candy Rehfeldt, who were my faithful readers, editing, offering sound suggestions, unconditional love, and true friendship. Thanks also to my editor and friend, Jennifer Stair, who has walked with me through the publication of two books, held my hand as we cut and edited, and encouraged me as a friend and writer. Her suggestions and skill helped bring this book to life.

I also want to thank my acquisitions editor, Amanda Soderberg, and Rachael Sweeden, director of operations at Tate Publishing, who believed in me and guided my hand as we walked through the publication process. Thanks also to Amber Losson, my conceptual editor, whose insight and attention to detail kept me on track. Her ideas and suggestions were the glue that held this book together. Her expertise and advice were invaluable.

Last but not least, I want thank my loving husband, Jim, my devoted sons, Lee and Darin, my daughters-in-law, Holly and Blythe, who have blessed me immeasurably, and my precious grandchildren, Jack, Lily, James, Strother, and Hodge, who have taught me to laugh, love, and see the world with eyes of wonder.

Life is a wonderful thing if you make it that way...
If you do things right and love the Lord, you'll be all right...
My secret is my Savior.
A lot of people don't know him, but I do. I love
him. He's going to keep on being my Savior.

—Eugenia G. Sanborn, age 114,
America's oldest living person in 2010

TABLE OF CONTENTS

part 4
revisiting holidays and church traditions

part 5
revisiting history

part 6
revisiting spiritual truth

INTRODUCTION: A LEGACY OF TIME, TREASURE, AND TALENT

> Therefore God exalted him to the highest place and gave him the name above every name; that at the name of Jesus every knee should bow in heaven and on earth and under the earth, and every tongue confess that Jesus Christ is Lord…
>
> —Philippians 2:9–11

Life has a funny way of grabbing you when you least expect it. At least that's how it is for me. Sometimes an experience or picture instantly touches the heart, resulting in revelation or insight. Other times, the process of repetition is the catalyst that changes behavior.

I'm a different person now than I was ten years ago. Like all living creatures, I'm in flux. Perhaps that's the process of aging or being a grandmother. Maybe it's the closing in of ever-creeping mortality. But while my timeline on earth has shortened, my message has crystallized. I think about life differently. My focus is on eternity—there is nothing else.

When I wrote *Generation G*, I was overcome with awe and wonder at being a grandmother.[1] Though joyous, I was not fully aware of the responsibility this position entailed. Today, being a woman who is not only faithful but savvy has become a responsibility I can't ignore. I have so much inside and so little time to share. Not to speak up would violate everything I believe in that is good and pure.

Long ago, I discovered that I'm better at writing than speaking. In the past, I've been guilty of too much foot in mouth disease. There's something about transposing thoughts to paper that brings clarity. More so than thoughts that travel directly from head to mouth. When I transpose ideas to thoughts and pen to paper, in time and with prayer, the Lord refines the words; the keyboard and God filter out the impurities and make it better.

The result is this book that evaluates and reflects on life in light of God and aging—a book about discovering meaning and purpose as a grandmother and as a woman of years. By using life experience and the spiritual journey, I'm better able to come to terms with my role on earth in terms of eternity.

The impetus for the book came from my deep concern regarding the decline of morality, values, and family in the world today. Like King Solomon, I desire to spare future generations the experience of a meaningless life apart from God. I used to think it was enough to live out my values and faith. But now I know that as part of the elder generation, I have a responsibility for modeling and mentoring this heritage to the next generation. As keeper of the faith and parliamentarian of history, as lover of the one true God, I must speak up before the world is shaped by a watered-down gospel and a revisionist history.

Two events propelled me to turn pen to paper: First, the past two years of speaking about *Generation G* introduced me to grandmothers whose stories have motivated me to articulate their dream of passing down faith to the next generation. Second, the untimely death of a friend clarified the fact that life really is fragile. His tragic death hit me full face and catapulted me into action. Bold and unafraid, he witnessed outwardly as well as in quiet ways through conversations, notes, and words. As I saw how his life counted, how his faith was strong and unwavering, I knew that he had left no moment wasted to build the kingdom. His life encouraged me to make a heartfelt evaluation of my own.

Convicted, I can sit on the fence no longer. To begin my reflection, I revisited my life themes in light of the spiritual context of eternity. I looked at the circle of life, specifically the fall season in which I now reside. I pondered not only the physical but the spiritual legacy I desire to leave. I reviewed nursery rhymes, fairy tales, holidays, church traditions, and history in light of God's truth. I revisited my spiritual life in light of eternity.

The result, *The Savvy Grandmother*, is a book based on the thoughts, observations, perceptions, beliefs, hopes, and dreams I experienced during these reflections. I feel a sense of urgency, for I don't know how much time I have left or what will happen. Only God knows.

I'm reminded of my favorite Chinese proverb, which says that "All the flowers of all the tomorrows are in the seeds of today." In that light I want to be a good steward of the seeds I've been given, my time, treasure, and talent. I desire to pass on these seeds in hopes that what I plant today will grow into fields of daffodils for my grandchildren tomorrow

I can't thank you enough, my readers, for your support. I'm certainly no grandmother expert, only a fellow sojourner along the path. But I pray that as we travel this road together, we'll remember, evaluate, and observe what God is doing. My heart's desire is that we all love from the depths of our being. That somehow we will each find a way to pass on our legacy of faith and make a difference in our time and generation.

As I reflect and give thanks for the gifts given, I'm aware that I am blessed beyond measure. I pray that my journey will challenge you to assess and determine your role and purpose. May this book inspire you to embrace the challenge of being a savvy grandmother. May it entice you to be a woman of wisdom who uses her time, talent, and treasure to leave a faith legacy and blessing for the generations.

part 1

revisiting the season of fall

MY HEART IS STIRRED

> My heart is stirred by a noble theme as I recite my verses for the king.
>
> —Psalm 45:1

There's no nobler theme than being a grandmother.

Grandmothering is the best—it's the only thing in life that is not overrated. For those who have not yet reached this noble pinnacle, in the words of Eliza Doolittle in *My Fair Lady*, "Just you wait."[1]

As Miss Doolittle experienced many layers in the process of becoming a lady, grandmothers, too, go through multiple layers in the process of learning how to make a difference in the hearts of friends and family. Like a seven-layer wedding cake, the sweetness of aging goes on and on. Just when you think you've got the hang of it, another grandchild comes along and adds one more layer of richness and discovery.

No matter how many books are written on grandparenting, the surface is only scratched—there is so much to explore and retrieve, so much knowledge and fun to experience. Before you know it, more layers are added to the repertoire, a suitcase already bulging with hidden treasures of sweetness and delight.

In my travels, I've had the privilege of meeting talented, creative women of age, many of them grandmothers, who are the backbone of this country. I am amazed by their stories of love, heartbreak, and triumph. Anyone who doubts the strength, per-severance, and determination of America need only spend a few hours with a passionate, savvy grandmother. Hearing her story and seeing the fire in her eyes will bring any believer to her knees. How could God plant such love in the depths of a heart?

We grandmothers are free to live in whatever way we choose. As each day brings an opportunity to make a difference in the lives of others, we also experience opportunities to glorify God's name. Our most important task in this season is to make an eter-nal difference in the lives of others, to live out our faith with those around us.

The Savvy Grandmother: Building a Legacy of Faith will help you discover how to enjoy the privileges and responsibilities of savvy, twenty-first-century grandmothers. As sojourners and daughters of the King, we not only have the opportunity to tell our stories, but we have the freedom to praise God for mak-ing it all possible. Now is the time for us not only to witness to His faithfulness but to be willing to give credit and glory to His Name.

Today there is a generation of godly women who live by faith and biblical principles, women who walk with the Savior daily, passing on the love of Christ and their faith to others. As savvy grandmothers, they compile and share their testimony and sto-ries, using them to inspire and encourage those who intersect their world.

To define a savvy grandmother is to describe a godly woman who knows the call of God on her life and acts upon it. Active, seasoned, and bold, she is a woman of faith, afraid of nothing except not spending eternity with those she loves.

One of the most important aspects of the savvy grandmother journey is healing our past in order to reconcile our future. Celebrating our own mothers and grandmothers is part of that task. By reflecting on and giving thanks for their lives, we are better able to heal our own past in order to reconcile ourselves for future generations.

Over the past few years, I've tried to do this. I have two sons and two amazing daughters-in-law who have blessed me with five grandchildren, four boys and a girl, ages two and a half to thirteen. Two grandchildren live within a mile of my house; the other three live just three hours away. Their presence in my life has added bittersweet moments of satisfaction and regret. Joy and sorrow intermingle as I reconcile my own journey in terms of past mistakes and lost opportunities. Reconciliation is possible through confession and forgiveness but only bring healing when reviewed through the prism of Christ's love.

In light of reconciling the past, our task is clear: sharing the love of Christ and the gospel. It's Jesus, pure and simple. Introducing those in our sphere of influence to our Lord and Savior is our goal. Sharing His love with the brokenhearted while stirring the hearts of friends and family is the noble theme to which we've been assigned.

Learning to tell our stories is a skill to be practiced, kind of like learning to dive off the high board. In order to dive into this freedom pool, we have to gather courage and take the leap. Diving off the high board as an adult takes the same amount of courage as diving off the high board as a child.

"One Brave Dude" is a trilogy in pictures that chronicles the journey of my grandson, Strother, as he took his first jump off the high board at age two and a half. A picture of trust and courage, it stands out as a metaphor for the faith walk.

In the first photo, Strother walks to the edge of the diving board, fear evident in his balancing arms and concentrating eyes. As he peers over the edge in the second picture, one can imagine the thought process of a two-year-old: *What am I doing here?* Kind of like when we peer into the unknown and ask, "Lord, are you sure about this?"

In photo three, Strother is suspended in midair, terror written all over his face. We, however, see from a larger perspective that which he does not yet see. There, in the water below, is his father, treading water, waiting with outstretched arms. He reaches out to catch his child the moment he enters the pool.

Isn't that how the Lord is with us? Standing with outstretched arms, our heavenly Father waits to catch us when we take the leap into the unknown.

Each of us has a testimony of when we jumped and how God caught us. A story of brokenness, we are witnesses to His outstretched arms, even in the worst of circumstances. Eyewitnesses to the power of forgiveness, our testimony stands as a model. By exploring new avenues of possibility, we can apply wisdom and biblical principles to the world and our families in new ways.

As I share my stories of faith, as I recite my verses for the King, I encourage you to recite your verses for the King. Think about your story, your God moments, your testimony of faith. Think about how you can praise and give God glory for the abundance and blessings of this life.

The journey is before us. We need to be packed and ready. So, grandmothers, arm the slides, as they say in airport lingo. Pack your suitcase and get on board. The plane is about to depart. Get ready to board and take the leap.

Getting ready for such a journey is a time-consuming endeavor, just as packing a suitcase. When I pack for a trip, I plan and prepare. Starting in the closet, I check one item at a time, making sure it fits my forever-expanding body. If it no longer fits, I give it to Goodwill or Union Gospel. Comfort items such as blow dryers, hand lotions, and hair gel are important to pack, but medicines, glasses, and comfortable shoes are necessities. The last step is to make sure that everything fits—a task of prime importance if one wants to be orderly, precise, and on schedule.

Packing our spiritual suitcases takes just as much time and effort as our physical suitcases. But one of the best-kept grandmother secrets is that our spiritual suitcases are already packed. They are sitting by the curb, ready to go. We just need to open and check them to see what's there. A lot of years have gone into these suitcases. They are bulging at the seams. We have added, subtracted, discarded, and saved an amazing amount of stuff, such as an overflow of life, laugher, love, joy, and tears. In fact, our suitcases are so full, they are close to overflowing. By checking it out, we may be surprised at all the wisdom they contain.

Checking itineraries is also important. By taking an inventory of how all theses items got into our suitcases, we move the process forward. Over the years, we have taken many dips and turns. Coordinating and organizing these multiple layers is vital if we want to have clarity about our journey.

Personally I can think of no greater gift than to open these suitcases and pour ourselves out onto others by breathing life, giving hope, bearing witness, offering encouragement, sharing the love of Christ, and being a mentor to our friends and acquaintances like Paul was to Timothy.

Yes, we grandmothers are prepared for the journey. Who knows the twists and turns we'll take? By discovering more about ourselves, we'll be drawn to opportunities where we can share the love of Christ, sometimes without even using words.

So let your heart be stirred; begin your song, review your story, recite your verses for the King. Get it down on paper or some other expressive form—paintings, quilts, scrapbooks, photography. Get it out there for all to see. For it's in our memories that stories become the springboards of faith for the world.

There is no nobler theme for the grandmother journey than leaving a legacy of faith. Reciting our verses for the King is a joy and privilege. Do it now while there is still time.

THE CHRISTMAS ORNAMENT

> The kingdom of heaven is like a king who prepared a wedding banquet for his son. He sent his servants to those who had been invited…to tell them to come, but they refused.
>
> —Matthew 22:2–3

Jim and I have been married forty-four years. It's hard to believe—we have almost half a century of history and memories together.

I have reminders of each year, thanks to a tradition we started the first year of marriage. Since purchasing a Christmas ornament on our honeymoon, we've continued to add more ornaments to our collections as reminders of special occasions and trips we've taken. Now when we decorate the Christmas tree, we revisit those times and memories.

Recently, we took a trip to the Hudson River Valley, the birthplace of Washington Irving, to see the fall foliage. There we purchased an ornament at the Washington Irving gift shop. I had no idea that such a small object would birth such a flood of emotion.

The result was this book about faith.

Describing the ornament is simple; explaining its significance, complex. A blue sphere, it depicts a tranquil country scene. I expected it to be no different than the other ornaments, inspiring me to relive and remember the things of the past. But this time, I was surprised by a dual purpose.

At first, the ornament reminded me of the passion I share with Washington Irving, America's first international best-selling author. But I did not expect the ornament to challenge and change my perspective on aging.

The shape of the ornament, a perfect circle, was the inspiration that birthed this book. I knew immediately that just as Irving's life came full circle, so, also, in time shall mine.

We all know that God is in the business of completion. Irving's life is an example of God's promise and blessing. As a young man, divine purpose intervened when President George Washington gave Irving a blessing at the age of six. Later, Irving commemorated this encounter in a small watercolor that still hangs in his home today. History records that Irving died at seventy-six years of age, just eight months after the completion of a five-volume biography on his namesake, George Washington—God's perfect circle completed.

As retirement looms and Medicare and Social Security forms are filled out, I'm reminded that the end is nearer than the beginning. I can't help but ponder what my full circle will look like and how God will draw all things in my life to their perfect conclusion.

In the past few years, I've had a paradigm shift. And although I remember past life seasons with fondness, I'm in a different place now. Like the Christmas ornament, my life is coming full circle.

I am no expert on aging, yet who could have known that in just ten short years, my perspective would shift from linear to circular?

The first fifty years represent the linear, when youth's energy built a family, gathered friendships, collected material goods, promoted a career, and planned for the future. These seasons of life were a big part of my transition toward the circular.

The circular began at the birth of my first grandson, one of my greatest joys. The transition is now complete. Life is no longer a straight line with a beginning, middle, and end. The remainder of my life's span has morphed into something eternal.

Completing the circle, I return to the beginning. Now I'm more focused on reflection, evaluating choices, looking at consequences of behavior, remembering loved ones, and meditating on what's really important. I ask such questions as: What is the meaning of life? What have I accomplished? Am I fulfilling my purpose for being here?

Rather than building, I'm divesting myself of property and material goods, simplifying lifestyles, letting go of expectations, grieving losses, and accepting the things I cannot change. From a spiritual perspective, I'm coming full circle, looking at kingdom values, biblical principles, God's promises, and the hope of eternity with new eyes. I'm preparing less for the world's kingdom and more for the heavenly kingdom. I'm focused on eternity.

I love this Christmas ornament, for it has been a catalyst to evaluate the seasons of life and has opened doors of the past to revisit and review. Developing a kingdom mindset, I'm evaluating the use of my time, talent, and treasure in light of eternity.

Scripture invites us to reevaluate and revisit. A friend and priest once said that Genesis 2 revisits the creation story and expands on it. That is what the Christmas ornament has done for me; it challenges me to revisit and review my story, seeing my life through a kingdom mindset.

I have a missionary friend who tells a disturbing story. When the Communists took over Czechoslovakia after World War II, she reports that they took God out of everything. Then they waited for the older generation, who remembered and knew, to die. Once they were gone, the young people had no tie to Christianity. Today, the Czechs have no idea what the beautiful cathedrals in their city symbolize.

Like it or not, we are the older generation. We will die sooner, rather than later. Where will our nation be then? Will our churches and cathedrals be the only reminder of a once faith-filled nation? What will happen to our world if we don't tell the stories of faith?

That's what this book is about: revisiting our past and using our gifts of time, talent, and treasure to glorify God by being bold in faith and passing on our stories of God's love and faithfulness to friends, family, neighbors, and future generations before it's too late.

When I was a child, faith was personal, a quietly held belief tucked close to the heart. My grandmothers were women of faith, but I only knew this by how they lived and by their word and deed. Although their faith was evident, it didn't need to be spoken; it was everywhere, in the schools, radio, television, and the public arena. Yet I miss that my grandmothers left no written word to pass on their stories of God's faithfulness. Today in this world of competing voices and philosophies, I wish I had a tangible expression of their faith to hold in my hand.

Surely our world needs the same. No longer can we rely on our quiet faith to be passed down, nor can we depend on our country to clearly state the message of Jesus. We have to take action. Like the Czechs, if we're not intentional, our faith will die with us.

I'm encouraged that it's not yet too late. As savvy grandmothers, we can make a difference. If we speak boldly, if we intentionally pass down our heritage and the stories of faith by using our gifts and talents, then we can proclaim Christ crucified and His love to those whom God puts in our path.

When I look at the Christmas ornament, I think of what was, is, and is to come. But most of all, I remember what is now. I remember Rip Van Winkle, one of Irving's most famous characters. A man trying to escape life and a nagging wife, he fell asleep before the War of 1776. Twenty years later, he woke to a different world.

Isn't that what's happening today? Too many Rip Van Winkles, asleep at the wheel? We've been busy with family, jobs, aging parents, and retirement. Now twenty years later, we're waking up to a different world.

Scripture prophesies this danger. Jesus says that people will be eating, drinking, and marrying, just like in the days of Noah (Luke 17:27); Jude talks of a church where scoffers creep in and sit among us (Jude 1:18); Revelation warns the church to wake up (3:2); the wedding banquet parable demonstrates the consequences of being too busy and disinterested (Matthew 22:2-14).

Thank goodness Scripture gives us the antidote—to return to our first love and remember that the kingdom of heaven is at hand (Revelation 2:4-5). The Lord Himself has planned a wedding banquet, and everyone is invited. He desires that no one be left out. What a travesty that one might refuse this invitation.

But just as in the wedding banquet parable, many today also refuse to accept Jesus's invitation. How or why is beyond me. Perhaps they don't know it's for eternity.

Let's not be the generation that falls asleep at the wheel. Let's wake up while there's still time. I don't know about you, but I want everyone to recognize the King, accept His invitation, and join the heavenly wedding banquet. I'm not willing to live with the unintended consequences of my failure to act.

The Christmas ornament has ignited a fire within. God forbid that I would leave unintended consequences in my sphere of influence for failure to act. We savvy grandmothers have been given a great responsibility. I'm convinced that this is the call upon our generation.

The Christmas ornament was my call to action. Our parents had World War II; our grandparents, World War I. Yet we do not fight against flesh and blood but against the unseen enemies in the netherworld (Ephesians 6:12). Who better to step out and take a stand than those of us who have nothing to lose?

As you read the stories and examples in this book, I pray that the Lord will plant seeds in your own heart, ideas you can imple-

ment by using your God-given gifts and talents to make a difference in the world.

And last but not least, may the Christmas ornament remind
each of us to revisit our own journey, that which we've been about
these many years. May we each view and restructure those areas
through a spiritual lens and a kingdom mindset. By taking the
love we've experienced, we can give encouragement and faith to
others, thus making a difference in our generation for eternity.

THE POWER OF INFLUENCE

> What we have heard and known, what our fathers have told us...we will not hide them from their children; we will tell the next generation the praiseworthy deeds of the Lord, his power, and the wonders he has done.
>
> —Psalm 78:3–4

How influential are grandmothers?

According to the Department of Commerce, there are 3.9 million children (6 percent) in the United States living in a grandparent's home, up 76 percent from the 2.2 million (3 percent) who did so in 1970.[1] I had three grandmothers, and although I only lived with them a short time, they were very important in my life. In fact, I am just discovering the full extent of their influence as I move further into the grandmother journey, especially as I struggle with the issues of aging and loss.

In families, a grandmother's influence, in or out of the house, can't be underestimated. When I worked as a therapist, many a session was spent with a woman sharing that her grandmother was the biggest influence in her life. There when needed, grandmothers love unconditionally and are great self-esteem builders. Strong in the face of storms, rocks in the midst of chaos, soft shoulders in times of sadness or disappointment, grandmothers leave their mark in tender ways.

In spheres of influence, a savvy grandmother's wisdom can't be discounted. Many a time I have sat in a meeting, debating an issue, only to have the oldest person in the room speak up. In one clear sentence, she sums up the discussion, bringing wisdom and resolution to the process.

As for the role of grandparents, Scripture is clear:

- "Even when I am old and gray, do not forsake me, O God, till I declare your power to the next generation" (Psalm 71:18).

- "One generation will commend your works to another, they will tell of your mighty acts" (Psalm 145:4).

- "Children's children are the crown to the aged, and parents are the pride of their children" (Proverbs 17:6).

Listen carefully to the directive of the Lord. Grandmothers are to mentor and teach the next generation, and that includes family, neighbors, young women, and acquaintances. We are to learn from grandparents. When we are old and gray, we are to not shrink back from our responsibility, but rather speak out and influence the next generation for Christ.

And that means all of us.

Whether you are a grandmother, have a grandmother, or will be one someday, the Word of the Lord has application for you. Only through time, effort, and prayer will we be able to discern what the Lord has for us individually. So let's get in the game and see what the Lord has for us in the area of grandparenting and aging.

For those lucky enough to still have a grandmother, you are blessed. Use this time wisely. Talk with your grandmother. Find out about her life and journey. How did she come to Christ? How has her faith sustained her through the tough times? If she doesn't believe, why not? What would she have you learn from her experience?

My three grandmothers and great-grandmother were all women of faith. Some of my favorite memories are of my great-grandmother, Gangy. Decked out in her Sunday-go-to-meeting clothes, she wore the same black dress, matching black high tops, and a black, veiled hat every Sunday morning. I knew that meant church, but I have no memory of words spoken to that effect.

My grandmother, Shakey, was a good and kind woman, and I adored her. Raising a family during World War I, the Great Depression, and World War II, she revered God and country. But what sustained her? How did her faith give her courage? I would love to know her stories.

Shakey was also a charter member of the sandwich generation. When I was only one year old, my mother and I moved into her home, along with my grandparents, my great-grandmother, my aunt, and two uncles. That's right, eight of us, four generations in one house! I don't know how she did it. What gave her strength? What wisdom would she have for me? How I long to have her here to glean from her experience.

All my grandmothers died before I thought to ask about their faith. How I wish they were alive today. I would sit down over a cup of coffee, seek their advice, and let them mentor me in the ways of faith. I know their life experiences would speak to mine in a personal way.

As grandmothers, matriarchs in a dark world, we walk a tightrope as we balance many balls. Facing a world that is unstable, ungodly, and more often than not immoral, most people are looking for a rudder, a captain of the ship to guide them as they journey forward in unchartered territory.

God is the only captain I would trust with my ship. How about you?

As occupants who have been sailing the seas of life the longest, we are in the position to introduce other passengers to our Captain. Many of us already have a seat reserved at his table. But do we invite our friends to dine with him and share His wisdom?

Do we bring our grandchildren to the table to experience the Bread of Life? Do we love on our neighbors' kids as if they were our own? Do we even know how close the Captain is?

Recently Jim and I took a cruise to Alaska on a ship named the *Voyager*. One of the side trips offered was a seaplane ride to a fishing camp, where we enjoyed fresh-cooked salmon over an open fire. Watching the fog roll in, it became apparent that the seaplane would not be returning to pick us up. Worried that we would not make the boarding deadline, we feared we would be left behind. After dinner, to our surprise and delight, eight helicopters appeared out of the fog, dispatched to pick us up and return us to the ship. Not until later did we learn that the captain himself was on the same excursion. He was right there with us all the time, and we didn't even know it.

Isn't that how we are? We often don't realize that the Captain is in our midst. Like this experience on the cruise ship, one of our guiding biblical principles should be the realization that the ship never leaves without the Captain at the helm.

Savvy grandmothers are in a great position to influence the world. Not only do we have life experience and knowledge of biblical principles, but we also have opportunity. What better legacy to leave than to pass on our faith? The more I've traveled around the country, the more I've discovered that one of my purposes in life is to exhort grandmothers to be intentional in their faith legacy. As grandmothers, we never know when an opportunity might arise to pass on our faith. When my grandson, Jack, was six, he visited for a week of Bible camp. Leaving every morning in his ninja outfit, he marched off to have water balloon fights and egg tosses, or so I thought. After four days, he came to me as I brushed my teeth.

"I want to say the prayer, Marme. Can we say it together?" he said.

At this point, I had never led anyone to Christ before, though I had planted seeds. I didn't know the five spiritual laws or the

Roman Road, so I had to depend on the Holy Spirit to guide my words.

I turned to Jack and asked, "What do you mean, 'say the prayer'?"

The camp had done their job; Jack knew exactly what the prayer of salvation was. With a clear understanding of salvation and forgiveness, we prayed a Marme version of the sinner's prayer, right then and there. I just followed God's leading and prayed. The Captain was closer than I thought, and my heart overflows to this day remembering the moment that my grandson came to trust Christ.

Grandmother sharing comes in all shapes and sizes. There are so many ways to pass on faith. Telling stories to young children is one way. Writing letters to older grandchildren is another. Giving a testimony at church or ladies' organization is a powerful motivator. Scrapbooking, quilting, and painting are creative ways to use our talent and tell a story. As gifts and mementos, they can't be overrated. The important thing is to be a daily witness to Christ. Giving children the gospel is definitely a powerful witness. What better gift to give a child than the opportunity to receive the gift of eternal life?

I remember Stan, who helped me with publicity for *Generation G.* Before its publication, I gave him a sample copy as a gift. He immediately sent it to his grandmother.

A month later he called. "Marty," he said, "I've got to have another book. I haven't read your book yet, but my grandmother keeps calling me to talk about it."

"Stan," I said, remembering my own grandmothers and what I wished I had known about them, "she doesn't want to talk to you about the book. She wants to talk to you about herself, to share her story with you. The best gift you can give her is to set aside time to do just that. Believe me, when you're my age, you'll wish you had."

What a testament to a grandmother taking action. I wish I could have been a fly on the wall to hear the wisdom that savvy grandmother passed on to her grandson.

My friend, Marie, is another grandmother whose boldness surprised even her. After I spoke at her church, she made a decision to write letters to all of her grandchildren, telling who she was and how she came to faith.

Her eyes twinkled as she chuckled. "I try to imagine their reaction when they received such a personal letter from their Nonna. Certainly this behavior is out of character for me. I'm thinking they're thinking that I've been diagnosed with terminal cancer, not long for this world, saying my good-byes. Won't they be surprised?"

I think of Barbara, who, when I spoke at her book club, shared that she has made it her life goal to make a scrapbook for each of her grandchildren when they reach the age of twenty-one. With much forethought, she weaves memories and scriptures together into a tapestry of a life lived and a life given.

Suzan is an artist friend whose discerning eye misses nothing. Recently she purchased an exquisite sculpture of three circles in an elliptical plane. Placing it outside her living room window, it has become an evangelistic opportunity as she explains the triune god, the one God in three, who created the universe and who loves us, using the sculpture as a visual to any and all who will listen.

If you are not yet a grandmother, don't shut your ears too tight for your job is to prepare for the role of savvy grandmother. Think about what you might want to leave your children and grandchildren, neighbors, and friends. At least look to your mother and mother-in-law, your own grandmothers, or a more mature Christian for advice. Open your eyes and ears. Keep a journal, make notes, and be clear about your own journey, what you want to pass down as a legacy.

Remember time is a great leveler; it moves so swiftly.

Keep in mind that young moms are often overwhelmed with diapers, carpools, schedules, and household chores. In my early twenties, I tried to balance four people into a twenty-four hour day, but the effort was exhausting. Often there was little left over to give. I wish I had lived near my parents or in-laws. I try to imagine what support they could have been. What better gift than letting the grandparents in your life help? Their presence is a gift, not only to you and your children, but to them as well.

If you are a mother with young children, celebrate the grandparents or older neighbors in your children's lives. Encourage them to develop relationships with your children. Wynette and Richard are the child magnets in our neighborhood. Always ready with a glass of lemonade and a chocolate cookie, kids from three to thirteen gather on their porch to laugh and talk. Look for ways to offer opportunities as a caring adult in order to be a part of a child's life. Even long-distance grandparenting can make a difference. I know many grandmothers who are dying to be involved but are waiting for the invitation.

Reading the Bible is the best place to get ideas. Studying God's call to mothers and grandmothers keeps us focused on God's plan for the family.

Our God is a great God. He created us to be reconciled to him and to one another in order to glorify him and to build his kingdom. Because of our rebellion, Jesus Christ became love incarnate so that we could be reunited with God. Only by allowing him to live in us are we able to offer him our hands, eyes, feet, and mouth for his use in the kingdom.

In a world gone awry, it is our only hope.

So get on the ship. Spend time with the Captain. Jesus is the answer. Let's join with Him and change the world for Christ.

UNDER CONSTRUCTION

Unless the Lord builds the house, its builders labor in vain. Unless the Lord watches over the city, the watchmen stand guard in vain.

—Psalm 127:1

Becoming a grandmother can be scary.

Before my first grandchild was born, I had no idea how to be a grandmother. But with each day, I have gained more confidence. On the first day of his life, I became a student, and as four more grandchildren have joined our family, the learning curve continues.

One is never too old to learn. I have heard it said that when learning stops, life stops. I can attest to this.

My mother and aunt are in their eighties, and they've never stopped learning. Recently they drove from Texas to Colorado to spend a week with me in our cabin in Lake City. We had a wonderful time. I want to be just like them, for their suitcases are overflowing spiritually, physically, and mentally. Disciplined with a ritual, they walk every day. Whether in the mountains or on the golf course, they get exercise. My aunt "swogs," a term she coined when she combined swimming and jogging at the same time. You can find her "swogging" three times a week in the summer. I've recently tried this myself and have found it more than worthy as a summer exercise addition.

My mom and aunt also play golf. In addition, they fish, bait their own hooks, reel in their catch, and even use needle-nose pliers to get the fish off the hook.

They keep their minds active with new activities and an edge of competitiveness. Every morning, my mom does the crossword puzzle in the newspaper. In the evenings, they play gin rummy or Boggle. I taught them Bananas and Rummikub and found them to be a formidable team.

My mom and aunt are still under construction. I am, too. Like them, I still have much to learn. Each day brings an opportunity to remodel, revamp, redecorate, or redo. If I want to be a worthy house for Christ, I have to keep this temple swept clean with continual upkeep.

As a young mother, I was a whirlwind of activity. Caught up in the world, secular in my views, arrogant in my beliefs, I was prideful about my capabilities. I was going to reinvent motherhood. I was determined to be different; I was certainly not going to be like my own mother.

When she came to visit, I resented her advice, closing my ears to her life experiences and wisdom. What was I thinking? In my zeal to do things my way, I was too big for my britches.

Funny how much smarter my mom became after only a few years.

Now that the blinders have come off, I watch her intently as she interacts with her own grandchildren. With my grandchildren, she is a great resource. When they are sick or troubled, she comforts. When she reads to them, she explains the concept in terms a child can understand. I grow more in my awe of her love and patience, her care and wisdom. I want to be just like her. Why did I not see it before?

I continually learn from her. Just recently at a family dinner, my mom walked over to Strother, looked him straight in the eye, and said, "I've been wondering about what you've been doing at school."

Eager to tell his stories, a litany of coloring projects and outdoor play came from his precious heart. As I watch her respond to his interest and presence, I see new areas to remodel in my own life. My mother has built her house on a strong foundation. Her values are sound; her faith is strong. Her life experiences make her teachable. She is a good student. Now she is in the professor role, modeling and mentoring. I admire her strength and excitement for life. In fact, at eighty-five, she got a new computer and transferred all of her financial records to Quicken and Word. Now that's a learning curve, even for me.

I finally get it—learning never stops. So today I am more teachable, more willing to take an honest assessment of my life, learning what works and doesn't work, what needs to change and be remodeled, what needs to stay as is.

Even as a grandmother, I'm still under construction. Like a construction site, it takes a team of builders—friends, family, church members, coworkers, and yes, grandchildren—to mold me into a usable vessel.

It's fun to be a house of many layers. In fact, the kind of house I am depends on my mood and season. Sometimes I'm a calm and quiet house, reevaluating, learning, growing, and changing. These are the times I pull back for reflection, the times I'm quiet before the Lord. At other times, I'm a whirlwind of activity. I gin and spin, taking care of four generations, a husband, a house, a career, and a spiritual life.

More often than not, I'm the same old me. I like the figurative house I live in, but I'm not above rearranging the furniture from time to time. Sometimes I change the paint color or buy a new piece of furniture that better fits my season. Often I remodel, changing old patterns and behaviors, which means teaching this old dog new tricks.

When Lily turned ten, we decided as a family to redecorate her room. Everyone participated. Scouring the catalogues and sales, we found a precious updated look that perfectly fit her personality. Now her room is pink polka dots and orange—a new look for a new season. She has entered the tweens in style.

Like Lily, I'm entering a new season in style. Recently I joined the "save the planet" campaign, purchasing two black canvas bags from Tom Thumb. Determined to save trees, I quit paper and plastic forever. Soon I purchased two more bags from Central Market. How could I show favoritism for one store over another? Currently all four bags hang on the closet door in my home.

Do I use them? Not yet.

My heart is willing, but my mind is weak. Old habits are hard to break. My biggest challenge is remembering to carry the bags into the store. They say it takes thirty times to break a habit. Hopefully, with time and intent I will be able to forge a new grocery bag habit over the next month. If I'm going to remodel myself for the grandmother season, breaking unhealthy or outgrown habits is a good place to start.

I'm also simplifying and divesting what I've got. Enough is enough. For example, I love to read, but I'm also satisfied with how my books are arranged on the shelves. So I've made a new rule. If I buy a new book, something has to go. Sounds like a good plan to me. Living a simpler life is certainly a behavior I want to model. How can I criticize excess if I'm the biggest offender?

Looking at the grandmother journey through the lens of a construction site metaphor really brings things into focus. Construction sites are great places to visit. Doing a walk-through of a newly constructed home, new ideas are generated to incorporate into my spiritual house.

But each construction site is different, as each contractor has his or her own style. At the end of the day, some sites are swept clean, all the equipment in place ready for the next day. Others are a mess with scraps of wood or tape and bedding lying about.

As grandmothers, we are in a building phase. In the early stages, we drew the plans and connected with the architect. Now, we're ready to build. How and what is determined by how much we've gleaned from the past and how much we're willing to give to the future.

Currently, my construction site is leaning toward the cleaning-up-at-the-end-of-the-day scenario, especially since I don't know what tomorrow will bring. That means cleaning up the messes in my life. The good news is, I have no deadlines. I'm in no hurry to finish, because when it's over, I realize the fat lady might well sing.

But boy, am I enjoying each phase of the construction. When I spend time with my grandchildren, I focus on them. No need to answer phones or clean the house or kitchen. I also love interacting with the children in my neighborhood. The days are short and the wonder large, and I'm in the middle of both. I love exploring their world.

A few years ago, I learned that grandkids have a sixth sense about things. If I listen with my heart, I can enter their world. When I stayed with my three Austin grandchildren while their parents took a trip, I had an opportunity to chat with James when he came home from kindergarten.

"What do you like best about school?" I asked.

"Recess," he said. "And guess what, Marme? I'm never going to be bad in school, 'cause I don't want to go to the principal's office."

"What happens in the principal's office?" I asked.

"I'm not sure," he said, "but I think you have to sit in a chair. You don't get to eat lunch, and you have to read a book."

Sounds like pretty bad punishment to me. James didn't know what happened in the principal's office, but how much worse could it get than not eating lunch and having to read a book?

The good news is that I didn't have to fix a thing. As a grandmother, I just got to listen to James's story and love on him.

Kids really do just tell it like it is. I hope in time I can be more like that as I pepper my own truth with a big dose of love.

When Strother was two, he had it all figured out. As I took him home after an outing, he noticed a car parked in front of his house. "Ladies at my house," he announced.

"How do you know there are ladies are at your house?" I asked.

"Car at my house; ladies at my house," he concluded. He'd already figured out the deal.

I'm glad to report that as the grandmother journey continues, I'm better at figuring out the deal and in a much shorter time than before. Like a child, I'm learning how to make my yes be yes and my no be no. I'm also learning to be intentional with my faith. Saying the blessing before meals has always been big in my family. Jim and I have been saying the blessing at every meal, whether we are with friends at a restaurant or the family at home.

Strother loves to say the blessing. When he was younger, my daughter-in-law reported, "You'll be pleased to know we're now saying the blessing at our house; Strother won't start dinner without it."

A legacy passed from grandfather to grandson—it doesn't get any better than that. Now we are taking the grandchildren to church.

Is that a hammer I hear—a Carpenter building his house? No flies on this savvy grandmother. I think my Under Construction sign has just gotten bigger.

SILVER HAIR, SILVER THREADS

> Remove the dross from the silver, and out comes material for the silversmith.
>
> —Proverbs 25:4

I am silver. No doubt about it—silver hair, silver heart. It's hard to deny aging when you're surrounded by silver.

Surely the Lord knew what he was doing when he allowed aging. So I'm trying to look at the process through his eyes. Rather than seeing aging as punishment, I imagine it as a monthly housecleaning by the great silver-polisher himself.

This is good news and bad news. The bad news is that I find a new wrinkle or silver hair every morning. The good news is that this morning once-over, reminds me that God is still clearing away the dross in the refining process.

We've all been refined in the refiner's fire. With time, a tapestry is woven that will only be complete when we get to heaven. I love this quote from *The Lacemakers of Glenmara* by Heather Barbieri: "Life itself is a thread that is never broken, never lost."[1] Everything we do counts for something.

We are threads, and God knows each and every one. Over the years, he has woven us into a tapestry. Many shapes and colors of wisdom weave in and out of our conversations and behavior, revealing a picture of who we are and where we have been.

The world has its own tapestry through the Internet, a global network that weaves the world together by invisible airwaves. Sometimes I think it's the modern equivalent of the tower of Babel. Each day, the Internet introduces a new gadget or game, a new way of connecting.

Recently, I discovered social networking, a form of communication that's alive and well in cyberspace. Somehow, through a small box, people interact with one another from all over the world. Photos and typed text form the basis of friendships that barely scratch the surface of real friendship, but the introduction of new faces and personalities grows our world.

The Internet has the potential to be a great power for good. Following the January 2010 earthquake in Haiti, doctor friends here in Fort Worth kept the world abreast of their work there through Facebook and other social networks. A whole community followed their progress, resulting in raised funds, needed supplies, a volunteer effort for months into the future, and a network of prayer.

No wonder the world is crazy for social networking. Connections abound, not only during disasters, but daily. Some of these networks are so sophisticated that with a click of a button, the thread of a conversation can be followed from its inception to present time. It doesn't matter what transpired in between; the thread of that conversation can be traced and revisited in the order that it transpired.

What a great idea. Wouldn't it be wonderful if we could click a button to follow the threads of conversations in our real lives? What themes would emerge? What surprises might be in store?

For years, I've kept a journal. It's not a diary but a chronicle of my spiritual journey, including the God moments, where the Lord meets me on a daily basis. All my successes and failures are recorded in this journal, the times I have been obedient and the times I have not.

Unfortunately, life does not play out in outline form. Everything in my journal is more or less jumbled together, a hodgepodge of good and bad, happy and sad.

At the end of the year, I try to make sense of it all. I need to see what God and I have been about in a visual way, so I mark the themes in red in the margins.

Wouldn't it be great if I had a "thread" button for my spiritual journal? Life would be so much easier. With the click of a mouse, everything over a year's time would miraculously be printed in outline form. Wow—what a time saver.

Despite my old-fashioned ways there's a method in my madness. Even without the thread button, the Lord speaks as the threads of his conversations are interspersed throughout the journal. I just need to figure them out.

November is the beginning of a fresh start in my journal. As the year comes to a close around Thanksgiving, I evaluate and take stock, redo, and discard. As I look toward celebrating the coming of the Christ child in December, I contemplate the threads and themes that the Lord and I have been about that year. Marking the successes and failures, the ups and downs, helps me prepare for the coming year.

Each year I try to do things differently. One year I made a gratitude list based on the threads I saw for that year. Seeing where God was working in my spiritual journal clarified how God was using me in the lives of others. Once identified, I could then be bolder in living out my faith.

Recently, my granddaughter, Lily, and I worked a bit on threads and themes. A slow starter in the morning, like me, she had fallen into a habit of dallying as she dressed and did her chores. Being a procrastinator myself, I am more than familiar with the issue.

One of Lily's favorite activities is storytelling, where she presents the characters and the setting, and then I tie them together.

Extremely creative in storylines, she often jumps into the meat of the story as well.

That evening, she set the story in her house with the main character Brownie, her stuffed monkey. Weaving the threads of procrastination and dallying into the story, I made Brownie the culprit and Lily the good guy. Before long, she was on board with the story. Using her problem-solving skills, we brainstormed solutions to Brownie's issues.

She's pretty quick. I'm confident she'll grasp the message and apply it to herself as she revamps and redoes her own behavior. In the past, she's been known to quickly correct the main character's actions, based on her own actions. I do believe she's a storyteller after my own heart.

Jesus was a master at using parables and stories to teach his lessons. So if it's good enough for him, it's good enough for me.

Storytelling is a wonderful way to communicate a point in a nonthreatening way and can be developed with a little practice. Some of my missionary friends report that they now use storytelling to bring many to Christ in foreign countries, for storytelling crosses cultural, age, and religious lines.

Not long after the first story, I told Lily another one. When she begged for more, I told her, "I'd love to, honey, but the story pocket in my heart is all empty. We have to wait for it to fill up again."

"I know about empty pockets," she chimed in. "I have some glue that after I use it, the bottle fills right back up. I bet your pocket'll fill soon."

Thirty minutes later, she tried again. "Is your story pocket full yet, Marme? I'm ready for another story."

Nobody is better than grandmothers at pouring out stories. But why not go one step further by sharing the gospel? Teaching Sunday school or Vacation Bible School is a great way to share Jesus through storytelling, a form children already know and love.

The trouble is, we procrastinate. We think there's more than enough time. But as we move forward in the journey, we discover that the grandmother season isn't all roses and light. Death and suffering abound. The further we go up the ladder the more we experience loss through tragedy or terminal illness. None of us can escape the storms of life. Relying on our faith to get us through is an action that speaks louder than words. Our great comfort is that God promises to walk through them with us.

My friend, Joe, tells a story about his friend, Maggie, who was a great writer. In her midfifties, she suffered a stroke and had to relearn to talk and write. Her rehabilitation was a struggle, but she was determined to write her stories. She died a few years later. Sadly, all the stories she was trying to get out died with her.

Let's not tempt fate. What a travesty to wait too long and have our stories die with us.

So I've stepped up my intentionality. I am more direct in my witness and more open with my heart. I'm identifying trends and threads that God can refine. I want him to make sure those threads fit into the big picture.

When I make that final journey, I want to leave no stone unturned. I want the picture I leave to be clear. I want there to be no doubt where I stood in my faith. I want my children, grandchildren, and friends to say that I was a woman who lived her faith every day of her life—even unto the last breath.

One thing I love about the Internet is the inspirational stories and pictures that come across my desk on a daily basis.

"The Cardboard Testimony" is one such story. The venue is some sort of stage with men and women of all ages holding cardboard squares. Each side represents contrasting positions of the before and after an encounter with the risen Christ. It doesn't take long for the viewer to get the picture: "Thief and Royal Mess"—"Now I'm God's Mess"; "God Robber"—"God-Led Giver"; "Sideline Christian"—"Now I'm Going to Be a

Missionary"; "Lukewarm"—"On Fire"; "Shackled by Anger"—"Restored by Love."

Contemplating a card testimony is a good exercise. Before I wrote my first book, I was focused on accomplishment and credit. But the Lord has a funny way of opening our eyes. Over time, in his disarming way, he has moved me from "credit seeker" to "glory giver." Once I wanted all the credit for myself. Now I just want to give God the glory.

Is God good or what? When God changes us, he changes us from the inside out. Silver hair, silver threads—what a beautiful tapestry woven.

IF THERE'S A MISTAKE IN THE PULPIT, THERE WILL BE A FOG IN THE PEW

> Preach the Word; be prepared in season and out of season; correct, rebuke and encourage –with great patience and careful instruction.
>
> —2 Timothy 4:2

In one way or another, we are all pastors. Like it or not, our audience is alive and well, sitting on our sofas or in our meetings as they take in every word we say and every action we deliver. As parents, grandparents, and active community members, we have a built-in congregation that lives in our homes and visits us more often than just Sundays. By taking the role of pastor seriously, we have the opportunity to correct, rebuke, and encourage in a loving, biblical way, using Jesus's example as our witness.

In light of *Webster's Dictionary*, which defines *pastor* as "a herdsman or a spiritual overseer,"[1] biblically speaking, we are all spiritual overseers of those in our sphere of influence. The word *pastor* comes from the Greek *pascere*, "to feed"—an apt description for a shepherd who watches over God's flock.

And isn't that what we do as grandmothers? We feed God's flock, those who come in our path with our life experiences, wisdom, discernment, and faith stories. We have responsibilities as pastors in real life.

A pastor in the pulpit has responsibilities, too. He's accountable for what he preaches and teaches. If he's grounded in Scripture, he will not lead his flock astray. If he feeds himself with the Word of God, he's more likely to stay in fields that are safe for grazing rather than drink from polluted streams. The Scripture tells us that if a blind man leads a blind man, both will fall into a pit (Matthew 15:14). If the pastor strays, we're all in trouble. We have seen this with pastors like Robert Tilton and Jim Bakker. Taken to the extreme, men like Jim Jones and David Koresh have pastored their flock unto death.

A pastor in the home has the same responsibilities. A mistake in the pulpit there can also lead to major destruction. A veil of confusion, a thick fog, or distorted thinking can fall upon a family in an instant. We all know families that have modeled unethical or immoral behavior and the consequences that are a result of their behavior. The expression "like father, like son" was not created out of nothing.

Consequences of pastors not being accountable to church authority are devastating. Again, David Koresh comes to mind. Without a proper chain of command, those in their pews often fall into the category of cloudy thinkers at least or muddled minds at best. Why else would congregations become distorted in their thinking and ill-advised in their actions? And why would they follow these men to such untimely and dramatic deaths or adopt a false gospel?

The Scripture tells us that if the church is not watching, scoffers will creep in and sit among us (2 Peter 3:3). And today in many churches, they have.

But flocks also bear the some of the responsibility. Learning to discern biblical teaching, to recognize the fog, requires some accountability. The same dictionary that defines *pastor* defines *fog* as "a state of confusion or bewilderment."[2] This is a great description for a congregation or a home that is led astray. Jesus often uses the metaphor of sheep and a shepherd for understanding the role of a person of God who leads others in spirituality, Bible study, discipleship, or theology. A flock of sheep that wanders off looking for greener pastures has either been abandoned by the shepherd, taught false doctrine, or is hard of heart. Either way, they are soon lost.

Parents, moms, dads, teachers, neighbors, and grandparents are also called to watch over God's flock and are responsible for those little ones placed in our care. Our responsibilities are enormous, and the possible consequences eternal.

Being grounded in Scripture and having a mentor are important for shepherding others in a Christian walk. As the parents go, so also go the kids; an acorn doesn't fall far from the tree. Children learn at the feet of the master—and that master to them is you. To have a healthy family, parents and grandparents need to be grounded in the Word. Only when we sit at the feet of the Master can we truly be useful vessels for his glory.

The truth is, we all make mistakes and get off track. Any pastor or parent who is truly walking with the Lord is quickly chastened when he gets off track by a friend, vestry, elder board, or by the Lord himself.

Laypeople are also chastened in many ways. Spiritual directors, mentors, or accountability groups are a good source of accountability. Mentoring others on a weekly or monthly basis helps steer a steady course. Many a pastor has lost his job because he failed to heed the warnings of the elder board; many a lay person has fallen because he did not listen to his accountability partner. Even pew sitters have been known to be challenged by small groups or discipleship partners.

I'm in an accountability group that meets bimonthly. When we get together, we share our lives and our walks. Keeping grounded in the Word, we are able to help one another stay accountable should we wander off the path, take the wrong turn, or move into the fog.

Recently, I shared my faith walk with them in regards to my writing. Listening with spiritual ears and seeing with spiritual eyes, they showed me behaviors in my own life that I was unable to see. Listening to their insights about my obedience and disobedience, I saw where I'd gotten off the path. There is something refreshing in confessing, repenting, and moving on.

A run-through of today's news headlines illustrates the importance of staying on God's path. Alternate lifestyles are on the rise. Polygamists, transvestites, cults, pornography, wife-swapping—the list goes on.

How will the children of the world, how will our children and grandchildren, learn to make wise choices if our generation doesn't share the wisdom of our parents and guide them when they are young? How will they learn to see through the fog if we don't equip them with fog lights? How will they see through the darkness without the light of the gospel?

I recently read an article in the newspaper about a child who was named Adolph Hitler at birth. He was correctly removed from his home by Child Protective Services. As a victim of distorted thinking, it was a tragedy for him but could be construed as an intentional act of abuse on the part of his parents. Not only did they wound him, but they named his siblings Aryan Nation and Heinrich Himmler. In my book nothing more need be said. The parents claimed they read these names in a book and liked them. But any way you look at it, ignorance is not bliss and can often be dangerous and destructive to others.

These parents were in a fog, deceived by the evil one himself. Clearly, they had never been taught right from wrong. Either way, mistakes were made in their home or church pulpit, for the fog in their pews was palpable.

As believers, we have checks and balances as we seek account-ability from trustworthy, wise believers. Checking actions with Scripture, seeking wise counsel, and brainstorming consequences are exercises worth noting.

Questions to ponder include:

- What am I modeling when I drink and drive?

- Do I take the Lord's name in vain? If so, what message is this sending my children, grandchildren, and friends?

- What movies do I watch and what books do I read? What values do the people around me glean from them?

- How well am I practicing patience and listening?

- Am I modeling a Christian lifestyle, or is my behavior no different from the world's?

Our job is to keep our children and grandchildren out of the smog of the world and bring them into the light of the Word of God. By clearing up the fog, God's ways and commands will be made clear.

part 2

revisiting the legacy

A SUITCASE ON WHEELS

> Fools mock at making amends for sin, but goodwill is found among the upright.
>
> —Proverbs 14:9

We are all a mess. As humans, we gather a lot of moss as we roll along.

Just by being alive, we collect not only physical but emotional baggage. Soon our suitcases are overflowing with unnecessary gunk.

A good example of the suitcase metaphor can be found in the travel section of any department store, the suitcase on wheels. In my younger days, suitcases had no wheels. If they were too heavy, there were porters at the airport to carry them. Today it doesn't matter how heavy our suitcases are; we can carry our baggage wherever we go. All we have to do is roll them along behind us. The important thing to note is that we are responsible for packing these suitcases, both spiritual and physical. Everything in our suitcase has either been lovingly or carelessly placed there by us. And a lot of it is careless junk.

Carrying junk around is definitely not a good thing. Our baggage gets heavier with each passing day. From years too numerous to count, our grandmother baggage has increased to such an extent that some of us are dragging around a couple of steamer trunks behind us.

Think about the mess we are leaving behind. Oh my. Someone will have to clean out our suitcases after we board the plane. Better it be us if we want to leave a clean slate for the next generation.

But emptying suitcases is easier said than done.

Jim and I love to travel. Over the years, I've developed an unpacking ritual that can be helpful in cleaning out emotional baggage as well.

Upon returning from a trip, the first thing I do is place the overly packed suitcase in the middle of the bed. Then I make piles as I unpack: dirty clothes, things to go downstairs, things for the bathroom, personal items. Before long, the suitcase is empty, and everything is ready to be transferred to its new location.

Wouldn't it be nice if we could do that with our emotional baggage?

Ah, but we can. Let's open our emotional suitcases and see what can be unpacked. It's hard, but let's begin.

The first stack to unpack is unresolved issues, those things we have not fully dealt with or put to rest in our lives. Maybe it's anger at a mother-in-law for something she said, resentment toward a spouse, disappointment in a child's behavior or attitude, or fear of the future.

One of my unresolved issues has been a failure to forgive. For years I've carried this baggage around in many areas of my life. Sometimes it resurfaces at the most inopportune moments. By opening up the suitcase and bringing it into the light, I can deal with it.

One of the major issues in marriage is unforgiveness. We each have incidents and memories that need a spirit of forgiveness poured over them. My marriage is no different. When Jim and I married, we were young and immature. Needless to say, we both made mistakes. As unforgiveness was stacked upon unforgiveness, we unknowingly built our house on shifting sand. When the storms came and the wind blew, our house could not stand. As the house fell, the marriage collapsed. By the grace of God, and in the spirit of repentance and forgiveness, our marriage was rebuilt on the rock, the solid foundation of Christ.

Once you've made a pile of "unresolved issues," the next step is to ask, now what? What will it take to resolve these issues?

Seeking the Lord's counsel is the first step toward healing. With time and prayer, the answer will come. This usually involves forgiveness or acceptance in some form, perhaps making amends on our part. If we have been holding on to something, it's time to let it go. If we need to make amends, do so. If there's something we can't change, then we need to accept it and move on. Taking a long look at each item will help put things in proper perspective.

Making a pile of "bitter roots" is our next assignment. Bitter roots are those negative feelings that have been buried deep inside and have now taken root. Perhaps it's an unforgiven marital transgression, a financial loss caused by a friend, a divorce, or a childhood wound.

Bitter roots call for deep scrubbing. Here's where we have to get down and dirty. The best and quickest solution is to get out the spot remover. Jesus in our hearts is better than OxyClean in our laundry rooms. We just have to fall on our face and confess our sins. The Scripture is clear. When we confess our sins, God is faithful and just to wipe the slate clean (1 John 1:9). Giving ourselves a thorough cleansing ever so often is good for the soul.

Our next stack is "unresolved grief," those things that we have lost or never realized: lost opportunities, dreams, failure to follow through, things we didn't try. Maybe we lost a loved one to death or had a business or financial loss. Maybe we had to move from an area where we were happy or were unjustly fired or accused of wrongdoing when we were innocent. Again, forgiveness plays a big role in the unresolved grief category. Acceptance is not to be ignored as we tread lightly through this minefield.

For years, I carried around unresolved grief regarding my parents' divorce. I blamed myself. This is not unusual. Statistics tell us that 50 percent of marriages end in divorce, so I suspect that there are many walking wounded carrying around this same unresolved grief. Forgiving others their shortcomings puts an end to the blame game. Remembering "There but for the grace of God go I" helps keep things in perspective.

Now let's unpack a pile of "lost dreams and expectations." As young brides and mothers, we had them. But things usually don't turn out as we plan. This is not a bad thing; it's just different. Maybe we thought we would settle in our hometown. Maybe we are childless but always wanted a big family. Maybe we expected to be the boss of a company but were passed over for a promotion. The truth is, if we hold onto these dreams too tightly, disappointment builds. This adds another bitter root to the garden we have been tending. Pulling these expectations up by the root prevents bitterness from choking out the fruit that God has planned for us in our life's garden.

I know a couple who couldn't have children, which was a huge disappointment in their lives. But with Christ's help, the Lord raised them up as cofounders of a nonprofit organization that works with children. Today, they have hundreds of children to love and mentor on a daily basis.

Next, let's look at the "discard" pile. This is usually a big pile, for most of us hold on to things far too long. I always recommend a separate stack for "resentments," for they are in a category of their own. As hard as we try, there are just some things we just can't let go, maybe that kindergarten teacher who never called on you or the neighborhood kid who made fun of you or a neighbor who didn't invite you to her Christmas party. Pull out these resentments, take a look, and then put them in the discard pile. Throw them out—the sooner the better.

Now for the fun piles, those things you want to pass down to your kids and grandkids. First are the values, morals, and faith that are so important in your life. What will you do with them? Take time for study and creativity so as to come up with the best solution. There are as many options as blades of grass in the front yard, so the sooner you start, the better able you're able to get a handle on it.

Next are the physical things in your home. I have a friend who has taped family names on the bottom of her favorite items. That way there'll be no question as to her wishes after she's gone. Others give away their valuables ahead of time or place a list of designated recipients in a safety deposit box.

We need to make a separate stack for personal things such as photos, heirlooms, letters, Bibles, journals, and spiritual books. What do you want to do with them? Once set aside and identified, they can then be creatively dealt with in due season, for now there's a plan of action.

And what about favorite scriptures and spiritual touchstone moments—what will you do with those?

Vera is a woman I met at one of my *Generation G* talks. After her mother died, Vera found a stack of journals hidden in a closet, over fifty years' worth. Vera didn't even know her mother kept a journal. She describes this find as a treasure. Every morning, she reads an entry from her mom's journal. She says it feels as if she is right there having coffee with her mom, all of her questions being answered.

We never know how or what God will do with these things. Debbie, my good friend and prayer partner, tells a story that shows how God can do the impossible. While cleaning out her grandmother's closet, she found her great-great-grandmother's prayer journal. She wept as she read the prayers her great-great-grandmother prayed over her great grandmother, grandmother, her mother, and a generation that was not yet born, Debbie and her sister, and their children. She has now passed these prayers on to her son at the celebration of his marriage. What a joy to discover that many of these prayers have come to pass in her generation because of the faithfulness of this great-great-grandmother.

See how easy it is to unpack a suitcase? Wow, I feel lighter already. I can walk around footloose and fancy-free now that I have set aside some of the items in that suitcase on wheels.

If I'm really on top of things, I'll donate that suitcase on wheels to charity so I can go about the business of living.

No more baggage for me—just gifts and fun stuff!

WHO'S PACKING YOUR PARACHUTE?

Guard what has been entrusted to your care.

1 Timothy 6:20

Years ago, a navy pilot was shot down over Vietnam and was forced to eject and parachute to safety. Many years later, a man walked up to him at a restaurant, shook his hand, and introduced himself as the pilot's "parachute packer." Assigned to the bowels of the ship in the Gulf of Tonkin, the man had carefully and laboriously packed parachutes for those above deck who flew tactical missions. His job was to make sure the pilot had a parachute and a way out if he needed it.

The truth is, we all have "parachute packers," those who undergird us while we are out and about the business of tactical missions for the Lord. Back in the 1990s, therapists referred to these people as *balcony people*, those cheerleaders and supporters who encourage and lift us up as we journey through life. After reading the story of the navy pilot, I was reminded of these balcony people. Since I'm committed to staying active in the twenty-first century, I've now replaced balcony people with parachute packers, and I'm having a lot of fun with it.

I think about those in my life who have lifted me up: my parents, grandparents, priests, friends, and spiritual mentors. They are the glue that hold my life together. I am the person I am because they took the time and energy to pour themselves into me, to pack my parachute with loving care.

Now as a grandmother, it's time to come down from the top of the ship, where I've lived most of my life, into its center. Now is the time to think about those whose parachutes I'm packing. Whom am I undergirding? Is there anyone I'm holding up? The answer: my kids, grandkids, women writers, and the young moms I mentor at church.

But being a parachute packer requires intentionality. Do I really pour myself out on those whom God has placed in my path?

I think of my granddaughter, Lily. At ten, she is more than precious. Full of life and laughter, she experiences joy with each new day. When she was born, I described her to my friends as a "child of joy."

When she was six, she once called my home from Austin. "Marme, where are you?" she cried into my answering machine. "I want to talk to you because you are not here, and I miss you."

Does that tear at a grandmother's heart or what? It certainly makes me want to pick up stakes and move closer to Lily and her family. But that's not feasible. Instead, I must be thankful for the times we have together. She grows so quickly. Scheduling time with her is one of the best investments I could make. Listening to her heart from the lower deck of the ship is my job.

On a recent family trip to Colorado, Lily announced, "I don't want to sleep in the same room with the boys anymore. They talk too much."

Being an only girl in a family of boys myself, I understood her frustration. But there is a limit to beds and bedrooms in a Colorado cabin. Sometimes, creative measures have to be put in place.

I gave her a tour of the available options. No one was more surprised than I when Lily chose to sleep on an inflatable mattress in the closet. Against numerous objections, I stood firm on what turned out to be the perfect solution. Lily slept better and longer than she had the previous five nights.

Clearly, I'm one of Lily's parachute packers. A parachute packer listens and pays attention. I love it when I'm there to help her with sleeping solutions, homework, shopping, or just buying her the things of the heart, not the things of necessity.

As a second grader, she often read for twenty minutes before bed. One night we decided to make her reading time more fun by inviting her dog, Daisy, into the room. With pride, she read until Daisy fell asleep.

My grandson, Hodge, is another whose parachute I gladly pack. He is a dynamo and so precious I could eat him with a spoon. A lover of sports, there isn't a ball he can't handle. At two and a half, he can dribble a basketball and handle a tennis racket like a pro. I love being with him.

Even when he didn't talk, he knew I was there for him. When I visited his house, he would squirm out of his mother's arms and run toward me as fast as he could. As I picked him up, he Velcroed his ear to my mouth, waiting expectantly for me to whisper sweet nothings, words of love from my heart to his. Even now, he asks me, "Come to your house, Marme?" I'm not surprised, because when he's here, he's the center of the universe. Sometimes I think he just likes to check out my snack drawer to see if I've hidden something special there just for him.

Parachute packing comes in many shapes and sizes. When he was one, Hodge stayed with me once a week while his mother went to exercise class. Then parachute packing was mainly physical, as I climbed the stairs behind him with open hands and arms, ready to catch him should he fall. But to someone in free fall, that's a pretty important job.

Now I think parachute packing is getting down on his level, listening to every word he says. Currently, he likes to get up early for "cewal, Marme." Jim and I fight to be the one to take him downstairs, as it is such a precious time. He chats away, sharing his world and his thoughts as we get a glimpse of his heart.

As I reflect on my God-given responsibilities, I focus on the opportunities that God might place before me. Aware of my need to listen with my whole heart and pack more parachutes, I become more intentional in ordering my day and prioritizing my life. As my energy wanes, my sense of urgency increases.

The best I can give my family and friends is time spent with a loving Father as he pours himself out on me. The more I'm filled with the Spirit of the living God, the more I'm able to pour out on them.

The Lord has been packing my parachute for years, and he's never let me down. I have yet to plummet to earth without a safety net or a way out. What the Lord has done for me, I can now do for my grandchildren and friends.

Of all my grandchildren, James, age seven, loves most to pray at night. A peace that passes all understanding comes over him. Last year, I chose the scripture 1 John 4:18—"perfect love drives out fear"—to pray for him.

By speaking the Word of God over him, as I pray about his day and thank God for the things he did well, we also ask forgiveness for the things he did wrong that day. A comfort that only his heart knows comes over him. I pray that I'm building a safety net for him should he ever need to jump out of a plane.

Sometimes parachute packers are just there. Not long ago, Strother called me and said, "Marme, I'm missing you. Can I come to your house today?" This was good news indeed, as the day before, when I asked him if he'd been missing me, he replied, "No."

Unfortunately, I had a prior commitment. "I can't right now, sweetie. I have a meeting downtown," I explained.

"I can go downtown with you," he replied. "I like downtown."

Thankfully, I was able to make a play date with him for that afternoon. That seemed to placate.

Parachutes are essential in life. Thank God for the swift hands and full hearts who willingly stay below deck, doing the work that will one day carry others into the heavenly realm.

Praise God that, like the navy pilot, I've been saved by the parachute of the Lord himself. As my journey narrows, I'm now ready to go out and pack those parachutes for others.

TWO ANGELS
AND A STONE

> You have made my days a mere handbreadth; the span of
> my years is as nothing before you.
>
> —Psalm 39:5

I love cemeteries. Always have, ever since I was a child. That may
sound odd, but it's the truth. I didn't experience a lot of death as
a child. In fact, I did not attend a funeral until I was twenty-one.
But my memories of cemeteries go way back.

It's understandable why cemeteries were a place of comfort
for me. They were calm, orderly, quiet, and peaceful. As a teen,
I learned to drive in a cemetery because my stepfather, Guppy,
thought that it was quiet, a safe place where no one would
bother us.

Cemeteries have many memories. My dad died when I was
twenty-four and was buried in an old cemetery in Dallas that was
surrounded by hundred-year-old trees. I used to take my children
there for picnics. His gravesite was shaded by one of those trees,
a tall oak. Sitting beneath its branches, I was reminded of God's
sweet covering over us. The branches inspired images of the loving arms of a father that reach close to hold and protect. I was at
peace there.

Later, that tree was split in half by lightning. I have since planted a pear tree to replace it, part of making amends for unforgiveness in my heart regarding the divorce. But it's just not the same. Now, instead of the long arms of the oak, the four colors of the pear are reminiscent of the sweet, but different, seasons of life. This brings me a different kind of comfort.

Whenever I travel, I visit cemeteries. Once on a family vacation to England, we visited cemeteries from Sussex to Yorkshire. From that time forward, my good friend, Anita, brought back pictures of cemeteries from her travels from all over the world. It has become a family joke.

I love history; I majored in it in college. The truth is, tombstones can be quite a history book as you learn about people and communities from visiting cemeteries. If a number of tombstones share the same year of death, this could indicate a war or plague. If a female and a baby have the same date of death or if a man is buried next to more than one wife, this may indicate death in childbirth.

Once on a silent retreat, I came across a cemetery, where I wandered around for about an hour. I prayed, meditated, and read the tombstones, wondering about all the people buried there. I pondered their lives and how short their time was here on earth.

I also thought about the lives of those in my life who had died. I wondered if they accomplished all they wanted. What about Guppy? My Dad? My grandmothers? Did their lives count? Did their lives and witness bring others to Christ? Did they affect the kingdom?

We just never know how God will bring things full circle. His grace is never too short that he can't provide answers. About twenty years after my dad died, in a serendipitous moment or a divine encounter, I found a box of books that I had stored after his death. Moving them from place to place, I'd forgotten I had them. In that box, I found his Bible and spiritual books. Sitting in a quiet place, I read of his faith journey during the last year of his life. What an amazing blessing, comfort, and gift.

This new knowledge impacted me greatly as I saw the healing power of the touch of the Savior on a lost life. Sometimes in our limited vision, we just don't know. What I do know is that all the lives and family that have gone before have affected mine in one way or another. I suspect there are many stories out there that also reflect God's grace and mercy. But like a father's lost books, they hold stories known only to the recipients themselves. Unless their stories are told, they are lost to posterity forever with their passing.

In my wanderings in that cemetery, I came across two angels and a stone marking a mother and child buried side by side. The engraving on the stone said, "Here lie two angels who lived but a breath but blessed life in its brevity." I pondered these lives.

The average life span indicates that we have only fifty to one hundred years at best. Surely most of the people in those cemeteries were not anticipating death. One day they were fine, and the next day, gone. How quickly it all went.

Recently I read Greg Mortenson's book *Stones into Schools*.[1] He talks of a companion in Afghanistan who shared with him the effect of war and death on his village and nation in a poetic and poignant way. Describing the sadness of memories, he remembers a friend who ate breakfast with him in the morning and was killed in the afternoon. Men in war are cognizant of the frailty of life; yet I'm sure that man didn't expect to die.

One of Jim's favorite expressions is, "There are no atheists in foxholes." I pray that this man knew the living Christ. If not, I ponder how people without faith face death.

We've all heard it said we should live today as if it were our last. I wonder if these men in Afghanistan did just that.

One of my all-time favorite TV shows is *Touched by an Angel*. I love thinking that God works in our lives—healing, reconciling, bringing closure, and drawing us to himself—even to the moment of death.

On one episode, the angel, Monica, befriended a homeless man who was mad at God for circumstances in his life. Passing judgment, Monica closed her heart to him before she knew his story. How often, I, too, pass judgment before I bother to listen to a person's story. God convicted her heart by bringing her to repentance. Begging forgiveness from the homeless man, she served him by washing his feet, which brought life to a heart grown cold. Never having experienced such love, he came to salvation because of her obedience. He died the next day.

Summer is a good time for reflection. Not one who likes heat, I spend my summer days cleaning closets, catching up on unfinished projects, and reading. Finishing my life well is one of those unfinished projects. If I should die tomorrow, what would my tombstone say? Will my life count for something?

"Thank You" is a Christian song by Ray Boltz[2] that tells of a man who dies and goes to heaven. There he meets people whose lives he touched when he was alive on earth. What a powerful image. It's humbling to think that one day we will meet those whose lives we might have influenced or who have influenced us.

Death is just a breath away. As the day draws near, Jim and I have discussed our funerals. It's a hard topic to broach, but we've concluded that there's something about having a marker, a tombstone, in the natural that is a reminder that you were here in the physical. There's something about being in a cemetery, an order to things, when family genealogies are played out on granite markers. I want a marker that if it doesn't say, at least implies: "Here lies one who lived...who loved God and family...who died. She did the best she could with the God-given gifts and faith bestowed."

As I think about two angels and a stone, I have a mental picture of a mother and child, joined together in life by a cord, united in death by the Spirit of the living God, the capstone of life. I like to picture the two sitting together under that tall oak tree in heaven, picnicking beneath the arms of a loving Father, surrounded by that sweet covering. I visualize them enjoying the sweetness of the fruits of heaven, joined by Jesus himself.

Two angels and a stone—a reminder that life is just a breath. So let's not waste a moment to breathe life before our resting place in a tree-laden cemetery is memorialized by a few words on a tombstone.

GETTING LOST COSTS

> The word of the Lord came to Jonah…"Go to the great city of Nineveh and preach against it, because its wickedness has come before me." But Jonah ran away from the Lord and headed for Tarshish.
>
> —Jonah1:1–3

Jim and I got a Garmin for Christmas. What an amazing marvel of science. Though we are still learning how it works, I understand that it will keep us from getting lost. What a relief! No more arguing over routes. No more battling maps. With the tip of a finger, we'll be able to find our way most anywhere on the planet.

That's really good news, because I know all about being lost; I've been there more than once. The importance of knowing where I am or how I am going to get there is a documented fact. Not knowing usually ends up in disaster.

Jonah knew a lot about being lost, too, and his wrong turn ended up in major disaster. That's what happens if you intentionally run away from God when he gives you an assignment. Before you know it, you look up and find yourself in the belly of a whale.

On a trip to Amarillo, I looked forward to a quiet time during the five-and-a-half-hour drive. Just what I needed to calm the spirit. Spiritual music was the order of the day, as well as keeping up with friends on the cell phone.

No surprise that while on the phone, I made my first mistake. Missing my turn in Wichita Falls, I turned north to Oklahoma instead of west to Amarillo. Luckily, it took me only five minutes to figure out what I'd done.

As I turned around, the Lord poured out a spirit of conviction. *If you don't pay attention where you're going, if you're too busy talking to others and not to me, you're going to take the wrong turn, get off the path, and miss the assignment,* the Lord reprimanded.

Hard of hearing, I mistook his reprimand to be about highway driving.

Two weeks later, I was on the same road again. You would think I would have remembered the way. My mistake came right outside Fort Worth. Blind to my own shortcomings, I once again pulled out the cell phone. This time, I almost made it to Oklahoma before I realized my mistake. I had to get out the map to find out where I was.

Where was the Garmin when I needed it? Consulting the map, I discovered that I had gone an hour out of my way. What started as a leisurely drive ended up as a mad dash to make a book signing. One speeding ticket and five minutes to spare, I braked in the driveway, leaving a trail of dust behind and a stressed out heart inside.

What a great lesson in life.

Some of us have to get off the path more than once to discover when we've made a wrong turn. Consulting the Bible is the only corrective measure that gives God's answer to our problems. But how often do we consult this biblical map?

This time, the Lord spoke louder. *You are not following directions. See how easily you got off track? Without constant supervision, you are in danger of getting lost.*

God was not reprimanding me about being physically lost; he was warning me about being spiritually lost. Using the natural to demonstrate how quickly I get off the spiritual path, he helped me avoid a future Jonah disaster.

Getting lost costs. Hopefully I learned my lesson.

Now God is my Garmin, for he knows the way. I check in with him daily, before I get out of bed. Using my Wichita Falls experience, I now have a litmus test to see if I'm on God's path or if I've taken a detour.

In Jonah's case, God had to use bigger measures. A whale is a pretty good indicator. It would certainly have gotten my attention. The "Welcome to Oklahoma" sign was enough of a signal for me.

I found myself in Nineveh while writing my first book. It's often hard for an author to describe what her book is about. At least it is for me. I finally had to sit down and do a thorough chapter by chapter analysis. By listing the secular and spiritual themes by chapter, and by going line by line, I finally began to grasp why the Lord had given me the book and what I was to do with it. I thought it was all about me. But it wasn't. It was about him. But like my drive to Wichita Falls, I wasn't paying attention.

Gradually, God's plan emerged. For reasons I don't understand, I've been given a platform to talk to grandmothers about the importance of leaving a legacy of faith. That is my greatest and by far most important assignment. Not only do I have a message, but I'm propelled to tell grandmothers, elders, and writers of the urgency and importance of this assignment.

I am just one of many called to Nineveh to warn people of impending disaster. As churches shrink and people leave the pews, as the gospel is watered down and infiltrated with New Age rhetoric, the world is spiraling out of control.

The days are short; night draws nigh. The message of the gospel is the only hope we have to save our world. Each day the light of Christ is stifled. Watered down to be politically correct, the gospel has gotten lost in the world of humanism and postmodernism, where tolerance trumps truth. The truth is, God's truth trumps everything.

As grandmothers and the elder generation, we are exhorted, directed, challenged, called, pushed, and shoved to pass on our faith while there is still time. I urge you—find a way. Do it now. Pass on your faith in ways that others can understand and will be remembered long after you are gone. The lives of others might depend on it.

Without God, those in your sphere of influence may only have a Garmin to keep them from getting lost. And a Garmin is not enough.

Getting lost costs not only you, but those around you as well, and that's a disaster with a high price tag.

WHETHER IT'S COLD OR WHETHER IT'S HOT

> This is how we know we are in him: whoever claims to live in him must walk as Jesus did.
>
> —1 John 2:5–6

I have a friend who writes a daily devotional. Each day when I turn on the computer, it is there for me in living color.

I remember the day I clicked on the heading and there it was—a word for the day. A statement in poetry that spoke volumes: "Whether it's cold or whether it's hot, we'll get through it, weather or not." Weather has always puzzled me. Just this week, the high was 85 on Monday, and by Wednesday, it had dropped to the mid-30s. Go figure.

My body can't figure it out. We grandmothers know that when the heat index is up and the thermostat jumps around, we're in a heap of trouble. When the weather gets wacky, there is more cause for alarm, as our internal thermostat goes haywire.

Body temp or no, this too shall pass. We will survive. Layering seems to be the answer: just put on and take off, and the body is happy.

Recently, I went to a SOMA (Sharing of Ministries Abroad) conference in Savannah, Georgia. Held in the basement of a beautiful historic church, the unseasonably cold temperature wreaked havoc with our internal thermostats. Those of us from the South were especially unprepared. Looking around the room, layers of everything from pashminas to throws, vests to overcoats, were the order of the day, as we covered ourselves with anything we could get our hands on.

What a great metaphor for the spiritual life. There are so many things happening at once, sometimes we are covered in whatever is handy. Often, there is so much raising and lowering of the spiritual temperature, it's hard to keep up. Sometimes we have to cover ourselves with whatever is available.

When I was younger, I would stay in a funk for days, maybe weeks, when something bad happened. These days, I might experience a funeral and a rehearsal dinner on the same day—my spiritual temperature going haywire.

Today, if I let things get me down, I am in danger of becoming an emotional mess. Life is moving too fast, and I seem to be along for the ride, hanging on for dear life.

The important lesson is that God is with us no matter what. We will get through. The part that faith plays in our response is a testimony to God's faithfulness that we can pass on to our sphere of influence.

My friend, Beverlee, taught me a lesson in spiritual temperature. Beverlee's son was to marry on a Saturday morning. On Thursday night, her ninety-three-year-old mother died. On Saturday at the wedding, I asked how she was doing. I'll never forget her words.

"Well," she said, "today I'm celebrating my son's wedding. On Monday, I will bury my mother and mourn."

Beverlee knew the secret of life. Was she sad about her mother's death? Of course, but she was not going to let it interfere with the joy of celebrating her son's wedding. It takes a very wise woman to be able to carry this off.

Beverlee is a savvy grandmother. I've learned a lot from her. If we let the hard knocks of life get us down, we'll miss the joy of celebrating the milestones in the life of family and friends. The older I get, the more people there are in my life that have ups and downs. I just have to roll with the punches.

My mother, who is in her eighties, once told me, "You know, my social life used to be weddings and parties. Now all I do is go to funerals. If I let that get me down, I wouldn't plan or do anything for fear I'd not be available. I've learned you just have to plan life. If it's interrupted, it's interrupted. Sometimes you just can't do anything about it."

Beverlee and my mother have great thermostats. They know how to read the spiritual temperature.

Jim and I have a small plastic thermometer that sits outside our bedroom window. Each morning I consult it so I'll know how to dress for the day. One day, I went to the window, and the temperature gauge was gone. What an inconvenience. I had to open the window to decide what to wear. Jim has been instructed to get a new thermometer posthaste. I'm sure he'll comply. We both need it for our sanity.

The same could be said of my spiritual thermometer. If I don't go to the Lord's window each morning and check his Word, I'll lose my sanity; it's best to have the Bible on the bedside table and consult it often.

Once while staying with my three grandchildren in Austin, their rabbit, Oreo, chewed through the telephone wire at the same time my cell phone died. Out of reach and out of touch, my spiritual temperature was all over the map. Not being able to communicate with others almost sent me over the edge. Thankfully, my Scripture reading for the day was, "Do not be anxious about anything" (Philippians 4:6). The Lord put his spiritual thermometer right before my eyes, so I could dress for the day in his robe of righteousness.

Sometimes life is cold and other times hot, but as savvy grandmothers, we can demonstrate this temperature gauge for our family and friends, not to mention our daily encounters. Hanging out our spiritual thermometer is a good way to influence others and share our faith that God's grace will get us through.

My dad used to say, "Keep on keeping on." When life gets hard and cold, we muddle through, knowing that with God, we can weather anything. God promises he will take us through to the other side. He is our barometer and our protector.

With a weather gauge like that, who needs a thermometer outside the window?

By putting on the Lord's robe of righteousness each day, we don't have to run away from Nineveh. And better than that, we won't end up in the belly of a whale.

Now that's a spiritual gauge I can live with.

GIVE US THIS DAY

Give us today our daily bread…

—Matthew 6:11

At a recent family dinner, James asked the following question: "Dad, why don't we pray at dinner like Marme and Big Dad do?" There was a moment of silence around the table as his words cut through my heart like a knife.

I had a momentary flash of insight as I realized that his situation is not unique. Too many families today are too busy to pray before meals. Statistics tell us that each year, fewer and fewer families sit down to a family meal. Sports practice, piano lessons, and business meetings all interfere with what once was the best part of the day.

When I was growing up, family dinners were expected. The time and place were sacrosanct. There were no fast-food restaurants and few activities after 6:00 p.m. TVs turned off and activities finished, families sat down to a home-cooked meal and discussed the events of the day.

After-school activities were practically nonexistent. Neighborhoods were safe with bicycles, roller skates, and swings. Most of us played kick the can, hide and seek, tennis, and red rover right in our own front yard. About ten children lived within a two-block radius, so we pretty much had the run of the neighborhood. But when the church bell rang at 5:30, we were expected to be home for dinner. Dinner was the time when families sat down together, bowed their heads, and gave thanks for their day. Conversation flowed. Many a current event was dissected and rehashed, with everyone weighing in with an opinion.

Dinner was also the place where children not only absorbed a healthy meal but also a healthy dose of their parents' values. Reinforcements came at Sunday lunch with grandparents and friends. In fact, every Sunday after church, my family dropped in on extended family or friends with kids our age. No NFL games or NASCAR races for us. Family time was in session.

Not so today. With both parents working, many families hardly take time to share a meal, much less share their day. Most days are so hectic that conversation is often limited to a few minutes exchanging information and schedules. It is estimated that kids spend about four hours a day in front of the television. *Good Morning America* reported a Yale research study that revealed young children are exposed to 642 ads a year, promoting cereals such as Froot Loops, Cocoa Puffs, and Fruity Pebbles. That is astounding. Whose values are the kids picking up anyway, the parents' or the TV's? Without family dinners, who is going to correct their misconceptions, and when?

I'm so blessed that my both my daughters-in-law have made family meals a top priority. I love that they sit down together as a family and talk out the day. I know my grandkids are getting a healthy meal and a healthy dose of values.

When my kids were growing up, we had family meals, but we didn't pray together. I now see the importance of this ritual. In fact, I look forward to the times I pray with my grandkids. I love it when James asks me, "Marme, pray Jesus." Prayer feeds the soul, even a young soul who doesn't yet understand.

Yes, the Lord feeds the soul. He is in the bread business. When God parted the Red Sea and delivered the Israelites from slavery, he led them into the desert for forty years. While there, he fed manna to them on a daily basis, his offering of faithfulness. Praying with a friend or grandchild in a time of intimacy or need is manna in the desert.

When I was in grade school, my friends and I joined the Bluebirds, a 1950s version of the Girl Scouts. Every year we toured the local Mrs. Baird's Bakery; it was our favorite activity. There's nothing better than the smell of fresh bread. Even if you didn't know it was a bakery, soothing smells from the windows poured onto the highway below. You just knew something good was happening in that building.

The Lord is still in the bread business. Like the smell from Mrs. Baird's Bakery, he wafts manna over us each day. But it no longer comes in the form of hoary frost on the ground. It comes as blessings and opportunities, God-moments that grace our day and fill our lives.

Not long ago, I began mentoring a girl at a local elementary school with a Christian group called Kid's Hope. A collaboration between the Christian community and the schools, counselors match at-risk kids who are participating in the program with a mentor. Studies show that having a stable influence for just one hour a week can change a life. The mentor's job is to be faithful and present, to love and encourage, to help with school work, play, and just be consistent.

When I met Sarah, I was amazed. The Lord's hand had matched me with one whose needs I have had experience with. She has been blessing my socks off, manna from heaven from a loving God.

I have so many stories to share with Sarah. How I wish that she had a dinner table that would undergird and cover her in her heart's desire. Although forbidden by law to speak of God, prayers are the best way I know to intercede for others, manna pouring out from a living God. All I can do is my best by giving Sarah my time during the day in the form of mentoring and God's cover at night in the form of prayer to feed her sweet spirit.

Grandparenting opportunities are around us everywhere. What better way to be the aroma of Christ in the lives of our grandchildren and others at the school as a helper, the dinner table in conversation or the bedroom in prayer?

Bluebirds, watch out. God and Mrs. Baird are still wafting over hearts and minds of children and grandchildren in our neighborhoods. By joining God's team, we, too, can be in the prayer and bread business.

part 3

revisiting nursery rhymes and fairy tales

THE THREE LITTLE PIGS

Here I am! I stand at the door and knock. If anyone hears my voice and opens the door, I will come in and eat with him, and he with me.

—Revelation 3:20

Who says a two-year-old has a short attention span?

Not so my grandson, Strother. When he was barely two, Jack and I took him to a children's production of *The Three Little Pigs*. Since he was so young, I was concerned that he would squirm his way through the performance, so I sat on the aisle, prepared for a quick getaway. Boy was I wrong. As soon as the lights went down, he sat on the edge of his seat and didn't move again.

For months afterward, he asked me to repeat his favorite lines: "Little pig, little pig, let me come in…Not by the hair of my chinny chin chin…Then I'll huff and I'll puff and I'll blow your house down." As I reflected on his ongoing obsession with *The Three Little Pigs*, I concluded that the experience had been a great spiritual opportunity for a grandmother, and I'd missed it.

My mind returned to the straw, wood, and brick homes, where each little pig ran for safety. In each scene, the door was the key. It got me thinking about doors and safety.

A door is an interesting thing. It can be an entrance to a house, school, office, or playhouse. Everyone has them; everyone uses them. We close the door to our homes to keep burglars out; we close the door to our hearts to keep people out. Doors are openings, controlled on one side allow movement between two places as quickly as possible. In other words, a door is the shortest possible path between two worlds.

Scripturally speaking, a door is the opening of the heart to salvation.

One of my favorite "door" passages in Scripture is Acts 12, where Peter is freed from prison by the angel of the Lord. In the story, Peter encounters two doors. The first, a gate leading out of the city, opens by itself. It is not until he is safely through that he realizes the Lord has sent an angel to rescue him. The second is at Mary's house, where all the believers have gathered to pray for him. He knocks and knocks, but in the excitement, they forget to open the door to let him in.

Isn't that how we are? Either we fail to recognize an open door that is from the Lord, or we knock at the door of hearts, but they refuse to open and let us in.

Google is a modern-day door to the Internet. With the stroke of a keyboard, information on most anything can be brought to the surface. Recently, I experienced a visual picture of the power of doors when I Googled "Webkinz" for my granddaughter, Lily.

Grandmothers will do most anything for a grandchild. On one of her "just me" visits, Lily asked me to take her to Target. She wanted to buy another Webkinz for her collection. Our assignment: purchase Hopkins the Elephant and Hippie the Hippopotamus. When we got home, we went online to go through the adoption process.

I am here to attest that Webkinz is a top-rate marketer, for they hook the child from the very beginning. Once the child has an account as a pet owner, she receives her own virtual house. She then gets an additional room on the Web site for each pet she purchases. Next comes the decorating, furniture purchases, room color, and favorite objects to customize the room specifically for each adoptee.

Adoptees then visit one another by traveling from room to room. Are you getting the picture? They time-travel through virtual doors. In order to get from one room to the next, they stand in a doorway. With the click of a mouse, they effortlessly move to the next room, kind of like Dorothy in *The Wizard of Oz*. With just three clicks of her ruby red slippers, she made a wish and was transported to another time and place.

In this fantasy world, doors are the key. Only by going through the door can one travel forward.

In the spiritual realm, doors are also the key. But the spiritual world is not fantasy; it is real, living, and active. Jesus tells us in Revelation 3:20: "I stand at the door and knock. If anyone hears my voice and opens the door, I will come in and eat with him, and he with me." In this verse, Jesus is talking about the door to the heart. When this door is opened, one finds salvation through the door of forgiveness and a personal relationship with the Son of God. An opening that allows flesh and spirit to move quickly between two worlds, the spiritual and the physical, this door is the key to eternity.

I have a favorite meditation that describes a door as having three hinges. What an apt description for the physical, as well as the spiritual. According to the reading, to really secure a door in the physical, you secure it with three hinges. The same is true with the spiritual; the three hinges are the Father, Son, and Holy Spirit. This Trinity is the stability that holds a person in place, advancing us to the next level. Just like the Webkinz, once we get the hang of it, we flow easily from one room to the next.

But what happens to a door that has no hinges, the person who has no spiritual foundation? We all know them—people who are abandoned, forgotten, or wounded, those who lean up against a garage or junk heap as they close their doors to the outside world. They are lost, wondering which way to turn next.

One year, my sons created a visual picture of this spiritual reality by setting up a photo shoot downtown in Rule, Texas. The contrast was startling. Once boasting a population of more than fifteen hundred people, Rule has now shrunk to three hundred.

The shot was staged on Main Street beneath what once was a real red light but is now a blinking light, with the deserted town in the background. Knowing that the past is a key to the present, the Lord, in some divine way, used this photograph to emphasize the importance of our ancestors as open doors to our history. Outside the door, one sees abandonment, desertion, and decay. But inside the door is the path to the heavenly kingdom, a land of love, forgiveness, salvation, and transformation.

Without hinges, the walk-through is impossible. Without the Trinity, salvation is impossible.

Looking at hingeless doors is a fascinating study for a hingeless door can't be opened. Without the ability to open and close, it is useless and falls to the ground. With no anchor, connection, or foundation, it can't stand. Hingeless people are the same way. With no anchor, they fall with the slightest breeze for nothing holds them up.

That's what happened to my marriage before Christ. With no hinge to hold our marriage in place, with no God in our lives, no Trinity, a strong wind blew our door down. You might say the wolf in *The Three Little Pigs* saw the weakest link and moved in. We held on for as long as we could, but the storm was too strong and our faith too weak. The door fell, and the abandoned street in our lives was exposed. Only after a separation were we able to jackhammer up the foundation and rebuild a new house on the rock of Christ.

A door without hinges is also rocky and unbalanced. You never know when it will collapse. When it does, the collateral damage is devastating. The same with an anchorless person; unaware and unenlightened, they often damage those with whom they come in contact.

My heart goes out to public figures, many of whom fall from grace in a media frenzy of publicity. Not to condone their behavior but like all humanity they fall, but in a most public way. Unfortunately, the collateral damage they cause is destructive and devastating.

Thank goodness our God is all about forgiveness. I wish all would experience the saving grace and forgiveness of Jesus Christ. Brit Hume of Fox News said it best when he was interviewed about Tiger Woods and his indiscretions. His comments could certainly be applied to any and all public figures. "Tiger Woods will recover as a golfer. Whether he can recover as a person I think is a very open question…I think he's lost his family… but the extent to which he can recover…seems to me to depend on his faith. He's said to be a Buddhist; I don't think that faith offers the kind of forgiveness and redemption that is offered by the Christian faith. So my message to Tiger would be, 'Tiger, turn to the Christian faith, and you can make a total recovery and be a great example to the world.'"[1]

You can't get a clearer message of the gospel than that—a word for our time. God uses those who stay in close contact with him to build his kingdom, just as in the case of Brit Hume. But the truth is, we all have opportunities to introduce others to the hinged door of Christ.

If we don't act in faith, then we are accomplices and a party to anyone who is an unhinged door. For a hingeless door is out of control; nothing stable orders its way. Without a Father who loves, a Savior who redeems, and a Holy Spirit who leads, the anchorless person is without form or stability. Without threefold support, we all fall.

So hinges are a necessary part of the spiritual journey. As believers, it is up to us to carry extra hinges wherever we go, for we never know when we might need to step in, prop up, or stabilize a wobbly door. By introducing people to the Father, Son, and Holy Spirit, we help anchor the anchorless to the Lord. By introducing them to the master carpenter, we help the hingeless attach to the firm foundation of life.

In a perfect world, we aren't three little pigs who live in pretend houses, but we all know about closed doors, and we've all experienced big, bad wolves trying to blow our house down.

That's where Jesus comes in. As the Savior, he anchors our doors to himself. As the master carpenter, he builds a flexible door that is hinged and that lasts. And he trains us, his apprentices, to work with him as he brings stability and purpose to hingeless lives.

ONE POTATO, TWO POTATO, THREE POTATO, FOUR. . .

Train a child in the way he should go, and when he is old he will not turn from it.

—Proverbs 22:6

How do you make decisions?

Do you sit down and map out a strategy weighing the pros and cons, the potential ups and downs? Do you seek counsel from advisers? Or do you jump in and pray that your decisions won't cause a catastrophe down the line?

Making decisions according to God's plan is the best way I know to prevent the ripple-down effect of consequences. I was reminded of the importance of good decision-making the other night when my grandchildren were arguing over a restaurant for dinner: Lily wanted pizza; Jack, Chinese; James, Mexican; me, hamburger. The decision was made by reverting back to the 1950s, when my friends and I made decisions using the old, but never-failing, potato game. Chinese won, but this experience reminded me that some decisions are too important to be decided by the potato game.

As parents and grandparents, one of our main jobs is to model good decision-making. Sadly, if our children and grandchildren don't learn this skill at home, the hard knocks of life will become their teacher. By imparting this wisdom to them while they are under our roof, we save a lot of heartache and grief down the road. But teaching decision-making requires sacrifice and hard choices.

Studies show that you can't be a friend and parent to a child at the same time. There is time for making friends when adult children are out on their own. But before that time, our role is to be a parent to the child. Too many parents today try to look and act like their children, disregarding the parent role of teaching and modeling.

But grandparenting is a different story. As a therapist, one of the things I observed in my practice is that good decision-making is a learned skill. Some kids get it intuitively, but the majority don't have a clue. They have to be taught. Learning about consequences, natural and set, is the best learning tool around.

Let's imagine a study of the different stages of child development. The first group in the study is toddlers, those who are at the age of beginnings. This is a great time to start the decision-making process by giving two simple choices—apples or oranges? red or blue? We help young children build self-esteem. Like a young bird in the nest, they need only worms and small bugs for nourishment. It doesn't take much.

Strother showed me the wisdom of this axiom in a simple dinner exercise. He was barely two when Jim and I gave him the choice of quinoa or white rice at dinner. He chose quinoa. Can you believe it? Sometimes baby birds will choose healthy in spite of themselves. Hodge, as the second child, always wants what Strother wants. So my strategy is to help Strother make good choices. He in turn, will mentor his brother. All I have to do is sit back and watch.

When children reach preschool, they move into the age of control. This bird is getting stronger, discovering that he has wings. Giving him a choice of clothes is a good way to encourage individuality.

James loves football jerseys. If he had his way, he would wear the same shirt over and over, and he does. Sometimes the color schemes don't even match. The challenge is how to keep him from wearing the same jersey every day.

The solution? Call in Marme. Who better to spend the afternoon purchasing a multiple-football-jersey wardrobe? Not only will he feel good about himself, but Marme has the time of her life spending a day at the mall with her grandchild.

Many a day, when my own sons were his age, I sent them to nursery school in stripes and checks because they had dressed themselves. I don't know what the teacher thought, but in my book, they were building self-esteem.

In elementary school, the age of reason takes over. Early elementary, grades one through three, is a great time to teach decision making while kids are still in the nest. At this time, children still want to please, so understanding and reasoning are easy targets. Once a rule is clearly stated and the consequences or punishment connected, the child can see the cause and effect of actions.

Lily learned this lesson when she attended her first birthday party at the roller skating rink. Excited to be invited, she announced that she did not intend to skate. Knowing that she might change her mind, I suggested she bring a pair of socks. When she declined, I grabbed some anyway. Upon arrival, Lily decided to participate and was thankful that I'd brought the socks along. This incident was a great teaching tool to discuss cause and effect, plus the consequences of not planning ahead. She caught on right away and I've watched her responsibility level grow the more she comes of age.

Late elementary, grades three through five, is the age of weaning. At this age, the young bird is eager to fly. Preteen is just around the corner, and there's a lot of flapping going on. Finding a balance between decision-making and defiance is tricky. This is a good time to start loosening up on the discipline and let natural consequences take over. Pointing out the results of bad choices or bad behavior, cause and effect can sink in. Grandparents are really good at this, but pick your fights carefully.

My grandson Jack, at ten, was into long hair, too long for my way of thinking. But I'm not in charge. Wisely, his father decided to save that battle for far weightier issues. After all, hair is temporary, an ever-changing medium. In time, peer pressure resolved the issue.

Middle school is the age when our little birds begin flapping their wings. The young bird is growing, and the wings are in fast-forward. Too young to be independent but old enough to think they know everything, middle—schoolers are definitely a challenge. This is when kids experiment. At this stage, many parents tend to give too much freedom too soon. Putting decision-making into a controlled environment can go a long way in forging healthy habits. This is a time when grandparents can be a safe sounding board.

Parent-peer groups are a great tool. By keeping in contact with the parents of friends and schoolmates, open lines of communication set an atmosphere of consistency with rules and a strong foundation for future decision-making. But parent peer groups are for parents, not grandparents. As a savvy grandmother, I realize my journey has moved beyond the role of parenting into the role of sounding board. I don't get to make those major decisions anymore.

Peer pressure is hard to deal with and starts at a young age. I heard from a young mom that her three-year-old was playing soccer because all his friends were playing. Weekends were a nightmare as they shuttled four kids to their different activities. I shudder to think of the peer pressure that lies ahead for this child.

For grandparents, coffee cliques and support groups are the best way to garner support for staying out of the parent's business. Venting in a safe environment with like-minded friends goes a long way in keeping us in the role of grandparent, not therapist or counselor. After all, our children have plenty of avenues for that.

High school is the age our birds start to fly. All of a sudden, their flapping wings have caught air. Kids, soon to be leaving the nest, are testing their wings. Soaring is their goal. This is the last chance to ground a kid, meaning give them a good foundation before they fly away. Not rescuing but allowing consequences is the best preparation for life.

Negotiated consequences are a great tool. When our oldest child was a junior in high school, my husband and I set strong rules for driving. After one infraction, we wanted a statement that would make an impression, so we announced a month's grounding from the car. He negotiated for one week, we settled on two. It didn't take long for the first infraction. There was no debate about the consequence, as we all had agreed upon the rules beforehand. The good news: even when they think they've won, the natural consequences take over. After only one infraction, he found that hitching rides and missing out on activities was too great a price to pay.

As grandparents, we get the best of both worlds when it comes to decision-making. Having been there, done that, we are now in the passenger seat, looking out the window and enjoying the view. We just get to do the fun stuff. Instead of instructing, we get to be in a supportive role.

Games like One Potato Two Potato are a fun way for grandparents to help teach decision-making skills to grandchildren. James loves games from Go Fish to Monopoly, from checkers to dominoes. He will play for hours if you let him. When he was younger, one of his strategies in Chicken Foot was to separate all of his doubles from the other dominoes and place them on the side. He then played them one after another. No one had the heart to correct him when he slapped the domino on the table and shouted, "Chicken Foot!"—expecting everyone to be surprised?

His perseverance has paid off, however. Now he is the family game champion. On his last visit to Fort Worth, we set aside a whole morning for games; "game morning," he called it. He won resounding victories, beating me four times at Sorry and twice at Monopoly. Games are clearly his forte.

Today, instead of "One potato, two potato, three potato, four," my grandchildren prefer Rock, Paper, Scissors to make decisions and settle arguments, but I'd like to think that One Potato, Two Potato from Marme got them started on the right track.

MIRROR, MIRROR ON THE WALL

Now we see but a poor reflection as in a mirror; then we shall see face to face. Now I know in part; then I shall know fully, even as I am fully known.

—1 Corinthians 13:12

Remember the Disney movie *Snow White and the Seven Dwarfs*? As a child, I was afraid just looking at the wicked queen. I had to shut my eyes and hold my fingers to my ears, just to stay as far away as possible from her grasp.

As a child, many things in that movie impressed me. But the one thing I understood was that the wicked queen was pretty self-absorbed. When the mirror's answer to "Who is the fairest of them all?" sent her into spasms of delight, I could tell she thought herself the queen of the heap.

But just as in real life, things change. As soon as Snow White entered the picture, the queen turned multiple shades of green. When the day came that the mirror told her there was another fairer, she raged.

Things went downhill from there. We all remember the poisoned apple. Sin had a foothold in her world. Like many of us, she rationalized that the end justified the means. She convinced herself that her plans to harm Snow White were not wrong. Wasn't being the fairest of them all worth the risk?

As grandmothers, we surely understand this scenario, at least falling from the fairest-of-them-all throne. Back in the days when we were younger, there was a time when we, too, were the fairest of them all. Remember male heads turning when you walked into a room? I do. And I wasn't even that good-looking.

But one day it all ended. I remember the day as if it were yesterday. I walked into a room, and no one looked up—no head turned, no eye lingered. Talk about a shock. Clearly, the fairest of them all had fallen from the pedestal. And it did not feel good. Not once, though, did I consider a poisoned apple as part of the solution. Taking it in stride, with just a little protest, I moved into acceptance, knowing that time marches on, and now it had marched over me.

Later, I had the opportunity to share this experience with friends over dinner. "I am getting old!" I wailed. "No one looks at women over fifty these days."

"Yes they do," the husband of a friend replied.

"No they don't."

But as my curiosity got the best of me, I added, "Who?"

"Men over fifty," he replied.

Wow—who would have thought? And I had no idea.

After all, looking good and being the fairest of them all is a top priority in the twenty-first century. Without knowing it, age has opened a door to what "the end justifies the means" is all about. As grandmothers, we just have to switch our priorities. Placing age over beauty is the first step.

My grandson Jack challenged my theory when he visited the following spring break. He is a delight. His insight and talent astound me. Not only is he a great athlete, but he is an avid reader. He loves karate, but if there were a black belt in computer, he'd have it.

I learned a lot about Jack that spring. Harry Potter was then his greatest hero. He absorbed the *Harry Potter* books in one fell swoop, claiming that he had the record for reading the most books in the least number of days.

I have read only one *Harry Potter* book. The story was spell-binding, but I was disturbed by the message. As a young mother, I probably wouldn't have given it a second thought, but with grandmother eyes, I could see the wolf lurking to eat up Little Red Riding Hood, and I was not happy about it.

On first glance, Harry Potter seems to have replaced Snow White as the fairy tale, or should I say wizard tale, of the day. To say I don't approve is an understatement.

The draw for kids is understandable, but the use of witchcraft, wizardry, spells, and broomsticks are cause for concern. Having been in Africa, where real witchcraft is practiced, red flags were flapping all over my map.

But I'm not the parent. The dilemma: how to let Jack know my concerns without challenging the authority of his parents. With much prayer, I asked God for an open door, if that be his will.

As always when Jack visits, we make a list of the things he wants to do. The challenge is to accomplish as many as possible before the week is out. Eating fried chicken and buying a *Harry Potter* book were at the top of the list.

As God would orchestrate, the two intertwined. While waiting for our order at a fried-chicken restaurant, the topic of Harry Potter came up. The Lord answered my prayer by providing an opportunity to share my heart, faith, and value system in one fell swoop. Twenty minutes was more than enough time to share everything from good to evil, light to dark, and the end justifying the means.

We had a great discussion. Jack brought up some really good points. I listened and heard his position, but my position came through loud and clear as well. At the end I told him that I respected his opinion but that I would not buy him a *Harry Potter* book because it was against my principles. He understood and accepted without question. It was an amazing conversation, and for an instant, I had a window into the mind and heart of my grandson. I was pleased to see that critical thinking is alive and well in his brain.

In a divine appointment over a drumstick, God allowed me to share my concern regarding the voices and philosophies that surround his generation. I told him how, in my day, everything in my life—family, school, church, and books—emphasized a message and value system based on biblical principles. He shared his perspective, which was more insightful than I could have imagined. Determining how to identify good and evil took us down the road of discernment, which opened a whole new door for discussion.

I felt good about our conversation but am still convicted about the need for prayer regarding this issue. God will surely have to undertake for this generation, for the darkness gets stronger by the day. But nothing is impossible for our God. I am banking that he will surround and undergird this precious one with light and truth. I pray that the seeds planted will grow into mighty oaks in the years to come.

My prayer was answered a few months later when Jack, on his own, but with what I suspect was the helping hand of the Lord, discovered the *Chronicles of Narnia* by C.S. Lewis. That started a whole new area of discussion.

The lesson: fairy tales are alive and well, but their message remains the same. So, buyer beware. Being replaced by those fairer and younger is not fun, but it happens to the best of us. As grandmothers, we are blessed to be a light in the dark to those very ones who are part of our own bloodline. Let's not be wicked queens who can't face the truth, manipulating and controlling in order to stay at the top of the heap. Instead, let's be instruments of the God of peace to be used for his good purpose as we plant, sow, and mentor the next generation.

"Mirror, mirror on the wall"—so much for being the fairest. I'll take older and wiser any day.

HUMPTY DUMPTY

"I am willing," he said. "Be clean!"

—Mark 1:41

Most children can recite the "Humpty Dumpty" nursery rhyme. There's just something about the rhythm and cadence that attracts children.

But what about adults? Do we ever read or meditate on the words and apply them to our world? If not, perhaps we should. Spiritually and politically, Humpty Dumpty is a prophetic word for our time.

Spiritually, we know that Adam and Eve took the first bite of the apple. As a result, sin entered the world. They fell big time. And God banished them from the garden. Thank goodness he had a plan for reconciliation and salvation to bring them back into right relationship with him.

But like Adam, Eve, and Humpty Dumpty, we, too, fall off the wall. And no amount of effort—no work, horses, or power—will ever make us whole again. Once cracked, the damage is done. Only God can put us back together. The Bible is clear about that. Forgiveness and wholeness come only from a loving father and his son who seek to reconcile us to themselves.

The Bible is full of living, breathing Humpty Dumpties. One of the most glaring is the Apostle Paul, a Pharisee who believed he was doing God's will when he persecuted the early church. On the way to more persecuting, he encountered the risen Christ on the road to Damascus. Once the scales fell from his eyes, God used him in mighty ways to bring about the kingdom of heaven.

And he can do the same with us.

A look in the political realm gives us great examples, Humpty Dumpties in every arena—so many cracks, so broken. Why we try to repair that which is broken with something that is more broken is a mystery to me.

The truth is that not only as individuals, but as a nation, we are flawed. Until all men come under the headship of Jesus Christ, no amount of effort on our part will solve the problems of pride, greed, arrogance, dishonesty, or distortion. Self-centeredness always takes center stage. The ego reigns when each man is king of his own fiefdom. When will we ever learn that Jesus is the only way?

The scriptures tell us that truth is a pearl of great value, a field of great worth (Matthew 13:44–46). When found, we must sell everything, go, and buy that field. Jesus is the truth. It therefore follows that we must give up all to follow him, for he purchased our fields at great price.

As a nation and as individuals, we need help. Many books, textbooks, and even some churches distort the truth of Scripture. As a country, we have lost our rudder, the foundation of a nation built on the rock.

In the Gospels and the book of Revelation, Jesus speaks to a sleeping church. "Wake up," he challenges. "He who has an ear, let him hear" (Revelation 3:2, 6).

If only we would listen.

Every day in the news, we hear of more scandals and darkness. As kingdom-minded grandmothers, a word spoken in gentleness and truth at a dinner party or a social affair might open a heart whose door has been closed.

If the heart is aligned with the father's heart, the ear will discern the truth. Recently, I heard a heated political discussion regarding Sarah Palin. In the midst of flaring tempers, a voice of reason gently spoke. "I like her," a friend said. "I may not agree with everything she says, and certainly she is fallen like the rest of us, but I find her refreshing. I love that she stands firm in her faith and walks out her beliefs."

You could have heard a pin drop. Who could argue with that?

The opposite is also true. If we listen carefully, the ear will discern falsehood, false doctrine, distortion, and deception. By paying attention to common sense, we go a long way in the discernment process while the world is still jumping around trying to decide which field to buy.

As savvy grandmothers, we're right in the middle of this Humpty-Dumpty, upside-down equation, for we know a lot about healing and repairing. We've experienced God's grace and forgiveness time and time again. We've been there, done that. We've seen his hands putting things back together. We've fallen, cracked open, and been put back together by a loving father.

Grandmothers know about hurt and woundedness. Nothing kisses a boo-boo better than a grandmother's lips. No arms are softer than a grandmother's when they surround and hold a wounded heart—or a grandfather's, too, for that matter.

Jim loves anything cowboy. Rod Steagall is his favorite cowboy poet. Discovering that he was in town during the Chuckwagon Cookoff on the Northside, Jim took Strother to get a book signed and bought chewing gum for Strother in the process.

Ten minutes after he returned home, the phone rang. Three-year-old Strother was on the line. "I need Big Dad come back," he wailed. "Big Dad took gum."

When they arrived at his house, Jim had quietly placed the package of gum in his pocket to keep Strother from over chewing. Strother could not be consoled. So his mom wisely handed off the problem to its source. Being the good Big Dad that he is, Jim got right back in the car and took that gum back for his mother to deal with.

Wisdom counts for something. As savvy grandmothers, we have seen kings come and kings go, but we know the truth. There is only one king—the real King. We know him, have met him, and need to tell others about him. In a safe, loving environment, children can be taught spiritual truths that will affect generations to come.

By applying "Humpty Dumpty" and other nursery rhymes to biblical principles, savvy grandmothers provide teachable moments. Explaining truths of the kingdom—the real kingdom—can impart truth and wisdom to the next generation.

Every three years, a church in our neighborhood puts on a play as an outreach ministry. The last production was *The Music Man*. What a powerful gift and witness to the community, not to mention the amazing performance by a church-only cast and crew, a performance worthy of Broadway. The musical's longtime effects are not tied to a limited run. By tying the unconditional, transforming love of Marion the librarian to the unconditional love of Jesus Christ, a powerful message was spoken over the audience. Love permeated that place from the stagehands to the ushers to the performers. Jesus was front and center. Hopefully, a curtain call for an encore was planted in the hearts of many.

Jesus is the real and only ruler. He has the power and authority of the reigning king. He also has all the King's horses and all the King's men at his disposal. He just has to say the word, and one is healed. Putting Humpty Dumpty together again with one word is a snap for him.

And we are all part of this ruling kingdom, for we are one of the King's men. Once saved and healed, it is our time to give back. Now it's our turn to look for other cracked eggs. Bringing the wounded and broken to the throne of the King is the job of the King's men. Healing them is the King's job. It's time for all the King's men to get off the wall and get to work.

As savvy grandmothers, let's arm ourselves with the weapons of the King. Let's take back the world for his kingdom.

JACK BE NIMBLE, JACK BE QUICK

Your word is a lamp to my feet and a light for my path.

—Psalm 119:105

"Jack be nimble, Jack be quick. Jack jumped over the candlestick!"

Can't you just picture it? A young boy in the eighteenth century, dressed in nightshirt and hat, sneaks out of bed in the middle of the night. Quietly, he places a candlestick on the floor. In an instant, over he goes.

A typical boy, so curious, so all boy. I have four grandsons, ages thirteen and under, and their behavior is not unlike Jack of the nursery rhyme. They're always asking questions, tasting and smelling, hearing and seeing, and doing the most unusual things.

Not long ago, Strother did a twenty-first-century version of jumping over the candlestick. Walking down the stairs, he announced his actions in advance. Hiding nothing, he held his sippy cup in both hands.

"Watch me, Marme," he boasted. "I can put this straw in my ear!"

And he did.

Now what goes through a boy's mind that makes him want to put a straw in his ear? What kind of curiosity wraps itself around a kid's brain that entices him to jump over a candlestick? You got me. Never in a thousand years would I think to do such a thing.

But to him, it was normal.

Strother came by this curiosity naturally. His father suffered from the same syndrome. Once, following a forty-five minute car ride, he exited the car and got down on his hands and knees to see what had propelled us so efficiently. With horror, before I could stop him, I watched his three-year-old hand reach out to touch the tailpipe. Second-degree burns were the result of his "jumping over the candlestick."

Under safer conditions, watching young boys push the envelope is one of my favorite pastimes.

When Hodge was ten months old, he discovered climbing. Back then, I caught him climbing into kitchen drawers, the bathtub, the wine rack, and the toilet. Learning to climb down the stairs backward was his greatest accomplishment. Now he climbs fences, sofas, beds, trees, and whatever else looks fun. So far, he's too young for candlesticks, but I have a feeling he's going to be jumping or climbing over a lot of them.

It got me thinking about how we are all Jacks, Strothers, and Hodges in one way or another. In spite of repeated warnings, we continually jump over candlesticks or put straws in our ears, much to the consternation of our heavenly Father. Sometimes we do much worse, like touching tailpipes. Like with Hodge, if we just look up, there is someone bigger at the next step to catch us if we fall. Don't you know God just shakes his head in his heaven at some of the things we do?

The Scriptures give just a hint of our rebellious nature.

Adam and Eve just wanted to taste the apple; look what happened to them. Jonah didn't want to go to Nineveh; he took a detour and had to be swallowed by a big fish to get him back on track. Lot's wife turned to a pillar of salt because she couldn't let go of the past. At the same time, Lot argued with God about how far he had to run to escape the fire and brimstone of Sodom and Gomorrah.

On the best of days, aren't we all a bit like these examples from Scripture? Call it curiosity or rebellion, each in our own way wants to go our own way. Rather than listen for the still, small voice of God, we'd rather test the water ourselves. Just like Hodge, who insists on dressing himself, opening his snacks and blowing up his floaties, we say, "I do it myself," over and over.

And he lets us.

So what can we do about it?

Surrender…surrender…surrender. There is no other way. Then watch for opportunities to help God build his kingdom.

On one of my early morning walks, I passed a sign in a front yard that said, "I helped light the lantern." I wasn't sure what it meant, though I later learned it was a capital campaign of some kind. But it reminded me that the Lord is in the business of lighting candles, not jumping over them.

We can learn a lot from "Jack Be Nimble," especially as grandmothers. Remembering that a grandson would rather jump over a candlestick than light it is our first clue. By guiding and mentoring, helping them light a lantern, we can show the way to eternity. By lighting the way for their rebellious hearts, we can start them on their journey to the Lord.

Family vacations in Colorado are great fun, especially when all eleven of us, plus two dogs, are together in one cabin. But bedtime is bedlam. Getting five grandkids bathed and in their pajamas takes an army, but we get it done.

No matter where they sleep, whether a bed in the bunkroom, a futon on the loft, or a blowup in the closet, they all ask for a nightlight. They know about the dark. If they wake up and need to get up, they want a sliver of light to light their way.

Isn't that how we are? We all need a sliver of light, one small candle by the bedside, one nightlight plugged into the wall to light our way. What better legacy than to light that lantern for a grandchild, friend, or neighbor, to light the way out of the darkness that leads to the Savior?

Jack be nimble, Jack be quick. No more straws in the ear or jumping over candlesticks for me. I'm going to Home Depot tomorrow to buy some nightlights. Then I'll be prepared to light a lantern when the opportunity comes my way.

THE SILVER BULLET

You are the light of the world. A city on a hill cannot be hidden. Neither do people light a lamp and put it under a bowl. Instead they put it on its stand, and it gives light to everyone in the house.

—Matthew 5:14–15

When I was a child, the Lone Ranger was a really big deal. Every Saturday, we went to the Ridglea Theatre to see what new crime the Lone Ranger would thwart next.

The Lone Ranger was my generation's equivalent of Superman. Eventually he became a TV icon, and we were fans for life. Even today, my heart beats a little faster when I hear the symphony play his theme song, "The Cavalry Charge," from *The William Tell Overture*. When I hear the words, "Hi-ho Silver, away," I am transported back to the days of yesteryear, to another time and place.

The Lone Ranger was a hero. There was no rascal too mean, no varmint too dangerous that he couldn't outsmart, outrun, out-hit, or reform. He was so good that he could wrap up the deal in a neat little package in just thirty minutes.

Often I find myself wishing for those days. It was simpler then, a time of safety, of ease and hope for the future. We never even locked our doors. The bad guys were somehow under control. Often, I find myself wishing for that simple faith. It's all so complex now. Today I'm wondering where all the Lone Rangers are, the heroes of law and order, faith and morality. Where are they when we need them?

To a child, the Lone Ranger was bigger than life. We all know that he is fictitious. But there is one who is bigger than life, and he doesn't need a big screen to reveal his purpose. Although the days are evil, Jesus is just a heartbeat away.

But so many do not take the time nor spend the energy to get to know him. The Scripture is clear. God will not be mocked (Galatians 6:7). He draws near to those who draw near to him (James 4:8). There is no problem, no solution, beyond God's means. And believe me, in today's world, he's very busy.

In January 2010, we saw the amazing pictures of the devastation in Haiti. But many do not know that while celebrities and politicians were fighting to land at the Port au Prince Airport, a cadre of doctors and health professionals silently made their way into the midst of devastation, saving lives, praying with families, bringing hope to many in the midst of their darkest hour. People were rescued, surgeries done with a minimum of equipment, hope and medicine dispersed. Out of the ashes, God worked miracles.

The Haiti photo ops are a sad testament to our times. I worry about the values being taught by the world at large. Jim and I rarely go to the movies anymore, because there is so much violence and explicit sex. Instead of Doris Day in *That Touch of Mink*, we get Glenn Close in *Fatal Attraction*. "*Que sera, sera*" has definitely taken a turn for the worse.

A kid's world is no different. On a recent visit with Jack, I had to revamp my agenda from outdoor play to indoor fun because of thunderstorms. Finding something to do became a challenge for this savvy grandmother, and I got the education of a lifetime. Everywhere, we had to contend with ratings—not just the PG and PG-13 for movies but for television shows—TV14, TVG, and so on. The video games had ratings of E, T, and who knows what else. I could hardly keep the initials straight, much less the ratings.

I guess ratings are helpful, but I can't help but wonder: how have we have fallen so low as to need ratings in the first place? The exposure on TV is enough to drive a sane person crazy. As parents and grandparents, how we can protect our young ones from the onslaughts of the world?

Every night I fall on my knees and thank God that I didn't have to deal with these issues with my own children. But my children do, and that makes me very sad. Today's parents have to deal with an ever-changing and corrupt medium that affects our families.

Parents have to be vigilant, much more than in my day. Round-table discussions and current events must be scrutinized and discussed, Scripture and biblical principles dissected, in order to give children scriptural grounding. Family meetings are my favorite way of talking things out in a safe environment. One year, when my three Austin grandchildren were visiting we had a daily family meeting to discuss the agenda for the day. They really got into it. Not only did we work out a compromise for the day's activities, but we had a lot of fun in the process.

There are many ways to enforce family values, but there is no one like parents—and grandparents—to do it. We can't depend on the government, the schools, not even the churches. It's up to us. It must begin in the home.

A few years ago, my brother had a quadruple bypass. It happened very suddenly while I was in Austin picking Jack up for his "just me" visit. As we came into Fort Worth, we made an unscheduled stop at the hospital.

'Why do we have to stop at the hospital?" he wailed. "I don't want to go to the hospital."

"That's what we do," I responded. "We're family. As family, we stand by one another in good and bad times. We have trouble here, so we're going to stand together as a family."

I've been able to watch this standing together as a family come to fruition in Jack's life. Every year, Jim has a roundup at the ranch to vaccinate and brand the cattle. This is truly a family affair, with Jack actively working with his dad, granddad, and uncle as they mentor him. He is learning to do his part in the family business.

Having a supportive church community, having a good relationship with neighbors, and being involved in schools is also part of this necessary equation. Back in the 1970s, Jim was in the air force. What a support system in action. We lived on base, where the kids could walk to school. Those were good years.

On a recent trip through Texas, we found ourselves thirty miles from our former home. Taking a detour, we excitedly planned to revisit that base in Oklahoma. Yet with the state of our nation regarding terrorism, and the increased security around our military, we were denied access. There was no Lone Ranger to vouch for us, to stand up for our character.

Taking responsibility for modeling Christian values is part of our job description. As Christians, our role is expanding in society. Needing not only to speak up for the importance of character, we now must also stand in the gap for others by covering our neighborhoods and schools in prayer. By volunteering in community organizations, churches and schools, by praying for teachers, principals, and government officials, we have the opportunity to be salt and light to others. How can we change the world for Christ if we do not permeate our environments with him?

Recently I watched a member of my aerobics class be a beacon of salt and light. During a break, as we panted over the water fountain, she threw out a question, "Anyone going to the luncheon tomorrow to hear Chuck Swindoll?"

A number of women gathered around. One asked, "Who's Chuck Swindoll?"

"He's a great Christian writer and a fabulous speaker. Would you like to come? I have some places at my table and would love for you to be my guest."

Wow— was she ever a light in the darkness in her small corner of the world.

The Lone Ranger was a light in the darkness in his corner of the world, too. Although masked, he righted injustice. As Christians, we are not masked, and we have the real Lone Ranger on our team. And he's not masked either. As his partners, we are able to stand out in our own sphere of influence, to breathe life and hope in the places we have been planted. With God on our side, there is no task too great, no valley too deep, that we can't be a witness and guide to a lost world.

Let's do it now. Let's make a list of places where we can shine. Mount that horse and charge full steam ahead!

Hi-ho Silver, away!

part 4

revisiting holidays and church traditions

DIRTY FEET

Now that I, your Lord and Teacher, have washed your feet,
you also should wash one another's feet. I have set you an
example that you should do as I have done for you.

—John 13:14

I have a game I play with my grandchildren. Bending over as far
as I can, I look them deep in the eye and ask, "Do you know how
much I love you?" Their eyes widen as they shake their heads no,
anticipating my response.

"This much!" I exclaim as I stand on my tiptoes, stretching my
arms as wide as they will go. "That's how much I love you—and
more! And you know what? God loves you even more than that!"
And then I give them a big bear hug.

They get the picture.

My love demonstration is simple, but it communicates the
height, depth, and width of my love for them, as well as the love
of Christ—a visual image spoken in the language of children.

In the world's view of love, Valentine's Day models the direct
opposite. A secular holiday, it grows in importance every year.
From January 1 until February 14, consumers are offered a
never-ending selection of hearts, flowers, candy, cards, and gifts.
Stores would have us believe that the size of love is measured
by the amount of money spent on gifts. A stroll down the aisle
at the Hallmark store reveals a plethora of choices. You name
it, they have it. Valentine's cards are now available for aunts,

friends, neighbors—any and everyone, just to let them know we love them.

Valentine's Day has turned into a secular holiday whose origins started with good intentions. The US Greeting Card Association estimates that approximately one billion valentines are sent each year, making it second only to Christmas in the card-sending category. I bet the retailers are having a field day on this one.

Don't get me wrong. I love Valentine's Day as much as the next person. Just like all consumers, I comb the racks for the perfect card. One year, I found a Barbie card for Lily, a Thomas the Train for James, a money slot for Jack, and a singing card for Strother. Hodge was still a gleam in his parents' eyes, so I could only dream for him. But even I know that if my words do not match my actions, the message of the card is meaningless.

Celebrating love is not new; it has gone on through the ages. But celebrating agape love—love that is eternal and unconditional—is something we grandmothers know and can do something about. We've lived it. We've been buried, burned, surrounded, and embraced by love. We have taken, shared, taught, given, and received love. We've experienced the different kinds of love. We know love that heals wounds and from whence it came. We've experienced the eternal nature that comes from the heart. We know that love is internal and intentional, a choice made to put another before ourselves. Love comes from the inside out.

If we know all this, why then do we not follow Jesus's admonition to love all the time? He states in John that all men will know that we are his disciples by our love. Clearly he speaks of godly love, not worldly love.

Jesus also tells us that if we love, we are to be a servant… that the last shall be first…that we are to wash one another's feet (Matthew 20:16, 26; John 13:14). These are hard teachings but worthy of a grandmother's ponderings.

Many years ago, five of us started a discipleship class at church. Being kinesthetic learners, we had an experiential exercise for everything. When we got to the chapter on love, we landed on foot washing. None of us had ever participated in a foot washing, so we had no idea it would be such a powerful experience. As we went around the circle, one by one, we washed one another's feet. Talk about a humbling experience.

Today I constantly struggle with how to go a step deeper in love. How do I model washing dirty feet in the midst of a world obsessed with germs? How do I instruct and model Christ like love, getting down and dirty, doing unto others that may or may not do unto me?

Jesus shows us time and again that he took on the role of servant to serve his disciples. In that day, washing feet was a custom performed by the lowest of servants. It should not be surprising that he calls us to serve others in the same way. Demonstrating this spiritual truth is one of the greatest gifts we can give others.

I have a cousin who took her three kids on a mission trip to Mexico. Talk about down and dirty. They had never served in the way they did on that trip. What better way, in a world of plenty, to give them an experience of true service?

Taking a look at dirty feet can bring clarity to our lives. A working definition of service is anything that does for another at some cost to me. In other words, doing a servant's job, putting ourselves second in whatever way is pleasing to or needed by another.

Recently I've noticed road signs with the words "I Am Second," a beautiful testimony to God written for the world to see. The famous and non-famous alike testify to God's supremacy in their lives. Would that we all lived a life that proclaims to the world, "I am second!"

Washing feet can take many forms. Savvy grandmothers could take a grandchild to the homeless shelter on Christmas or Thanksgiving to serve. Setting the table is another good way to start with young children. Even Hodge, at two, loves to set and clear the table. I "do it myself" comes in handy in these situations. The earlier one starts serving, the better.

Mission trips are also great opportunities to serve, as is mentoring or volunteering for Convoy of Hope or Habitat for Humanity in neighborhoods. Recently, a friend organized an extreme house makeover for missionary friends. Believers and nonbelievers alike participated in this outpouring of the love of Christ.

When it comes to spiritual love, I plan to talk less and to demonstrate more. Looking for opportunities to tell Bible stories that use life situations will catapult me into biblical teachings. Seeing with spiritual eyes enhances the application process.

Last but not least, I once again resolve to be bolder in teaching the good news of the gospel. "For God so loved the world that he gave his only begotten son" (John 3:16). *The Book of Common Prayer* says it so much more eloquently than I: "He stretched out his arms upon the cross, and offered himself in obedience to (God's) will, a perfect sacrifice for the whole world."[1]

Jesus stretched out his arms with the big "I love you" and gave us the biggest bear hug ever in the form of salvation and forgiveness of sins. This type of love is hard to understand. Jesus's love is so big, so deep, so wide, that he laid down his life for us—is that a foot washing or what?

MARCH FORTH

> The Lord will march out like a mighty man, like a warrior he will stir up his zeal; with a shout he will raise the battle cry and will triumph over his enemies.
>
> —Isaiah 42:13

March is a cold and blustery month. It blows in like a lion and goes out like a lamb. You never know what to expect in March. One year, a snowsuit might be the only thing that keeps you warm; the next, shorts might be needed to adapt to an early heat wave.

As grandmothers, we are a lot like the month of March. At least I am. As a young mom, I definitely roared like a lion. Full of energy and wildly protective, I stalked around, pouncing on enemies and friends alike. I saw predators around every corner that if not dealt with, might potentially upset my environment. I kept my den clean, weaned my cubs, and trained them for the battles of life. I was constantly on point for potential danger from the outside world. As I aged and they grew, I took to lying in the sun and guarding the pride, for there was much yet to be done.

Perhaps you identify.

Today, as I approach the end of March, I'm a lamb. It's comfortable and easy. Over the years I've mellowed, as I'm gentler in word and deed, certainly calmer, content to move and graze slowly, enjoying the field in which I'm placed. I like the grass before me. I do not feel the need to move to greener pastures. I graze and enjoy right where I am. No more stalking for me.

No more plotting and planning. I'm content to let the Lord lead and guide, to shepherd me with his presence and the touch of his crook.

I like living at the end of March. Actually, I was born in March, the fourth to be exact. My friend Janina says that my birthday is a sign, a commission from the Lord. "March forth," she says. "March forth for God's glory and his kingdom."

I like that; I hope it's true. Janina is one of my "parachute packers" who encourage me in my call. I like thinking that I'm commissioned to "march forth" in pursuit of the building up of God's kingdom.

As a grandmother, this commission fits now more than ever. As a seasoned sojourner and Christian, I don't feel militant, but there are glimpses that I'm becoming more zealous and perhaps a bit more radical in my passion for the Lord. Scripture says to neither look to the right nor the left (Deuteronomy 5:32), to take the Lord's yoke upon you and learn from him (Matthew 11:29), to take up our cross and follow him (Matthew 16:24), and that unless you become like little children, you will never enter the kingdom of heaven (Matthew 18), so I guess my glimpses are scriptural.

My passion grows every day. There's a fire in my belly that won't go out. If I take a look at the calendar and review the obituaries, I know that there is not much time left. What will I do with the time allotted to me? Where will I spend my energies?

As I ponder these realities, I realize that "marching forth" involves a gathering of like-minded souls. So where do I find these people?

They are everywhere. This is God's army—the believers and followers who seek to do his will and further his kingdom. They are the community into which God has placed me.

I was privileged to speak at a woman's conference in Connecticut, with many believers in one place. It was heartwarming to join these godly women as they gathered to worship and praise the Lord. With the joy of the Lord, they came together with singleness of purpose: to pray for our country and the Lord's will for it.

These were amazing women. Just by rubbing shoulders, "as iron sharpens iron" (Proverbs 27:17), our faith and the knowledge of the presence of God were sharpened. Their presence made me realize that I'm not alone on my journey.

There I met Kathy, who had memorized the gospel of John and was putting it to music. Barbara, a grandmother of four, recycled her grandchildren's receiving blankets, sewing them together and appliquéing scripture. Her grandchildren now have a physical reminder of her deep love for them.

As a member of God's army, my age and status in years puts me front and center. Surely that counts for something in leadership. Learning the skill of leadership is important, for I have a small platoon of children, grandchildren, neighbors, and friends who either walk along beside me or follow behind.

The Lord gives the orders. As I ponder mine, I have many questions about my journey. Have I taken the easy route? Am I walking down the narrow path, or am I stubborn and hardhearted, taking shortcuts, getting bogged down in a mud pit? Do I drag others along, or am I listening to the voice of God as he passes on the wisdom of the ages to the next generation?

I'm trying to stay on God's path as I follow my biblical compass and the map spread before me. I pray that I'm leading the way by my words and actions and that all around me see who I am and what I stand for. I want them to know what general I follow and where I get my orders.

Recently I went to the funeral of the mother of a friend. People of all ages were in attendance to honor MoMo, a woman of faith, known by young and old alike. During the service, her granddaughter eloquently shared the ways MoMo had touched her.

MoMo lived a life of faith. She taught her grandchildren to pray kneeling by the bed every night. She wrote letters of encouragement to friends and grandchildren, sending Bible verses, spiritual poems, and inspirational pieces. Each of her grandchildren had a MoMo file, and I suspect many friends did as well. Quotes from her letters and notes revealed a picture of a lady of faith, a savvy grandmother who was godly and unabashedly bold. She did not shrink from her call but left a legacy that is now being passed down to the third and fourth generation.

MoMo's actions inspired me. Although I keep in touch with my friends and grandchildren by e-mail, there is nothing like a handwritten note for posterity. I have therefore resolved to send more handwritten, personal notes and letters. I want those in my sphere to have something tangible to hang on to after I have passed from this life.

Last Valentine's Day, I picked a scripture passage for everyone in my family and for some of my friends who needed uplifting. I wrote the verse in their valentines. I have been praying this scripture over them every day all year long. Now I am putting them in a file for future reference. When I am gone, just liked Debbie with her great-great grandmother's prayer journal, I want them to see the scriptures and prayers I have been praying over them.

I am also sharing my commission to "march forth" with all grandmothers. I hope that you will adopt it as your own. As March blows in, be reminded to march forth for the kingdom. Be bold, be relentless, a zealous warrior. Be a lion.

As March breezes out, march forth as a shepherd for those baby lambs placed in your care. To be the lamb of the Good Shepherd, to hear the Master's voice and follow him, is the best gift we can give our families, friends, and neighbors. To mentor the baby lambs placed in our care to the best of our ability is a commission worth fighting for.

WHO DO YOU SAY I AM?

> But what about you? Who do you say I am?
>
> —Matthew 16:15

Music warms the soul and fills the spirit. A universal language, it speaks to young and old alike. From traditional hymns to contemporary, from classical to renewal, man has always expressed his search and love for a creator through the sounds and words of prose.

Some of my favorite songs are sung during Eastertide, such as "Hail Ye Festival Day" and "Christ the Lord Is Risen Today." In all of Christendom, there are no songs more uplifting than those celebrated on Easter morning.

How I love Easter, the time in church history when Christians celebrate Jesus's victory over death and sin. We are blessed to receive his resurrection power with the coming of the Holy Spirit. Most importantly, this is the day we celebrate the fulfillment of God's plan for salvation and mankind. There is no better way to tell the story than to sing it.

How Easter morphed into a celebration of eggs, bunnies, and chocolate rabbits, I'm not sure. I see no connection between Easter and the Easter Bunny. But come he does, with dyed Easter eggs and a basket filled with chocolate candy. Why does the world not recognize the secular nature of this false doctrine? You would think the natural consequences of cavities and stomachaches would garner attention. Unfortunately, the eternal consequences go completely over the heads of most. Either people choose not to believe, have closed their hearts, or do not know because we haven't told them.

What an opportunity for Christians to speak out as we cement ourselves in the saving knowledge of Jesus Christ and the redemption he brought to the world. What better time than Easter to share that as a people, we have all rebelled? But that God, in his infinite mercy, desires to reconcile himself to us. That's why we celebrate the Easter season, because he sent his Son to earth to bring us back to him.

Peter and Martha were not ashamed of the gospel. They were clear as to who Jesus was and his role in salvation and redemption. In Matthew, Jesus asks the disciples, "Who do you say I am?" Peter answers, "You are the Christ, the Son of the living God" (Matthew 16:15–16).

Later in John, Jesus asks Martha if she believes. She replies, "Yes, Lord…I believe that you are the Christ, the Son of God, who was to come into the world" (John 11:27).

These are two of my most favorite verses in the Bible. For Jesus is not only asking Peter and Martha this question, but he will one day ask every person on earth the same question. Who do you say I am? No one will escape. The application, then, is how will you answer?

I confess that there were many years when I didn't respond as a Peter or Martha. In fact, I didn't even know how to answer that question. It was not until I came to Christ as my personal savior that I had a response. But even then I only whispered to a select few that he was the Christ.

What was I thinking?

Now, everywhere I look, I wonder, *Do you know? Have you heard the good news?* What can account for this enthusiasm?

Perhaps it's age, perhaps a sense of mortality. I know that suffering the loss of many loved ones has had an impact on me. I can't explain it. But I've got the gospel bug. I want to share my joy and am looking for as many outlets to plug into as I can.

Technology amazes me. Whenever I buy a camera, iPod, or Garmin, it comes with about one-hundred-and-fifty cords and plug-ins as attachments. Who knows where these go? But you have to have a number of outlets to plug them into so they will function.

As a young mom, life was much simpler. In fact, I carried only one plug on my person, and that was to my family and busy life. Everything worked off the same circuit and used 110 watts. I was the user who plugged in or out of as many things as I could handle. I owned them; they didn't own me. It was nothing like the mess of cables today.

Now the youth of today are owned lock, stock, and barrel by all their gadgets and plugs. I can't help but notice that sometimes they have cell phones, e-mail, iPods, and who knows how many text messages going, all at the same time. On a recent overseas mission trip, I was struck by the silence on the airplane. What used to be a flurry of activity was now an enclave couched in silence. When I investigated, I discovered that every chair had its own TV and remote. With the flick of a finger, one could watch a movie, look at TV, watch a documentary, learn a foreign language, listen to music, or play a game. Of course, it was too much for me. I could never even get my screen to come on. I finally put the remote down in disgust as I reached for the well-worn, tried-and-true paperback book.

I'm glad I don't understand all of the bells and whistles. I'm glad I still rely on only one plug—the great power source himself. If I were one of those who relied on technology, I would be saying, "Stop this world; I want to get off!" In fact, there was a Broadway musical with that title back in the 1960s. Set against the backdrop of a circus, a merry-go-round gave a visual of life at the circus. Throughout the play, Littlechap, the main character, continually searched for greener pastures as he became more and more dissatisfied with life. Each time life got too hectic, he bailed, getting off the merry-go-round for something better. Sound familiar?

That's what's happening today. No commitment, no long-term connection, hunger for the latest gadget and plug, too much bailing out. Too bad no one ever made the connection—little chap, big God.

"Stop the world!" should become the mantra for the fast-paced twenty-first century. Most parents are in a tough position. It's hard to keep the good news of the gospel separate from the secular celebration of the Easter Bunny. Most parents are riding two merry-go-rounds on this one. Luckily, there are savvy grandparents who can slip into the Easter-go-round without batting an eye. We know the truth. Since we are once removed from the carousel, we are not afraid to expose it.

Being creative and bold is the name of the game. Giving and reading books on Easter is a good way. Christian bookstores have all kinds of scriptural teaching aids that bring the true Easter story alive. One year I gave Easter eggs that were filled with Christian symbols such as the crown of thorns, the cross, and the cup to grandkids and neighbors. Great discussions resulted as each egg revealed the hidden treasure inside. Through this simple tool, I was able to share in simple terms that even a child could understand.[1]

Peter and Martha knew who Jesus was and proclaimed him as the Christ without hesitation, with boldness and courage. Are we willing to do that? Are we willing to take a stand in our offices, families, and social environments? How about inviting a neighbor to church on Easter Sunday? The main question is, are we willing to state that we celebrate Easter because the Son of God came to earth to die for our sins?

That would be bold. For today, far too many churches preach a watered-down gospel that doesn't include the importance of sin and repentance. Others are heretical, as they do not teach the inerrancy of Scripture or the Sonship of Christ. Many tell us, "There are many paths to heaven…Jesus was a great prophet and teacher…All of God's prophets are equal…There is no sin."

This is not the gospel. Too many Christians believe with their heads but do not proclaim with their mouths that Jesus is Lord. Don't you think this Easter would be a good time to start? As savvy grandmothers, let's get off the world's merry-go-round and get on God's carousel. Let's be Marthas and Peters, proclaiming the good news of the gospel to the world.

Who do you say I am? This Easter let us proclaim Jesus the risen Lord.

Let us shout with a loud voice, "Lord Jesus, you are the Christ, the Son of the living God!"

NAVIGATING DARK TUNNELS

> Even in darkness light dawns for the upright, for the gracious and compassionate and righteous man.
>
> —Psalm 112:4

I love Holy Week. The daily readings of the Passion of Christ place the believer in the thick of the crucifixion experience, reminding us of Jesus's amazing sacrifice for us.

I thought I'd seen everything. But this year, Jim and I attended our first musical Tenebrae on Good Friday at a Bible Church. What a powerful experience!

The Anglican Church where I grew up always had a service on Maundy Thursday. It was very moving, but I never knew why I left with such a sense of hopelessness. In the service, everything that relates to Christ—light, candles, Scripture, and crosses—are taken off one by one to be replaced by emptiness. I didn't realize at the time that this was a Tenebrae service.

Tenebrae is a Latin word meaning *shadows* or *darkness*. A Christian service in the Western Church, it is celebrated in many ways by Roman Catholics, Episcopalians, and Protestants. The common denominator involves a gradual extinguishing of candles while readings and psalms are chanted or sung.

If you haven't attended a musical Tenebrae, you must. At the climax of the performance, with the choir sounding like angels from heaven, Jesus moves toward the crucifixion. As the candles are extinguished one by one, the auditorium is left in total darkness. The significance of the extinguished light is not lost on the audience.

What a visual picture of a spiritual truth. Without the light of Christ to permeate the dark, all truth and hope are blotted from view—total darkness.

I don't know how many of you have ever been in total darkness. I have, and it's scary.

There is a train in Europe that runs between Austria and Italy. For a fee, a car can make a reservation that takes a shortcut through the mountains, on the back of a flatbed train. In the convenience of one's car, a train carrying its load winds through a dark tunnel. Much like a ferry on water, the winding mountain drive is shortened by hours.

I knew that tunnels were dark. But inside the car, on top of that flatbed train, I wasn't prepared for such darkness. At one point, I insisted that we turn the light on inside the car just so I could get my bearings. The whole experience was disorienting.

Isn't that how we are in the middle of a spiritual crisis? When we are in a dark place, it's darker than we anticipated. Yet God is the engineer of our train. He can navigate us through any tunnel. We just have to trust, knowing that we are in good hands, for he has promised light at the end of the tunnel.

While in the tunnel, disorientation often takes over. In that case, there is only one thing to do. Turn the light on, reorient ourselves, and look for the light at the end of the tunnel. Only by turning on the power are we able to find our way.

What a good word for the twenty-first century, especially for mothers and grandmothers. Keeping dark tunnels and trains front and center in the mind go a long way in keeping us focused.

Trains can be a great teaching tool. In fact, James has always loved trains. Even as a child he favored *Thomas the Tank Engine* over *Dora, Bob the Builder,* and *Sesame Street.* He's gone from Thomas the wooden train to Thomas the electric train and loves nothing better than setting up the track. The only problem is that Thomas sometimes gets rambunctious and comes off the track. We then have to find a way to finagle him back on.

Isn't that how life is? Sometimes the track we're on is difficult to navigate. Our only choice is to get back up and get on track.

Another example is watching the Olympic Games. Time after time, an athlete will be knocked down or out, only to get up and begin again.

The past few years, as I've moved onto the grandmother track, if I let myself, I'd be overwhelmed by the totality of this current darkness that we call the world. The tunnel that will impact my children, grandchildren, friends, and neighbors for years is before us. It is dark and scary, and the train is moving forward at break-neck speed. I have no way to stop it.

The world is, indeed, a dark place. Only with Jesus and the indwelling of his Holy Spirit will light come back into this place. But how to tell the world this truth when no one wants to hear?

We know that with God's grace and plan for redemption, Jesus was crucified and raised from the dead. With his resurrection power, those of us who are his are the lights of the world. We stand on a hill, at the mouth and the end of the tunnel, shining a light into the darkness. As his body, his people, we are his hands, eyes, feet, and mouth. No matter how small our effort, we bring his light into a dark world.

As a grandmother, I've seen a lot. I know a lot. I have a voice, but it will only go so far. When one doesn't see, they just don't see. Resorting to discernment and prayer are my best options. Seeking the Lord in all things and speaking up when led, my influence as a grandmother and a woman of years can make a difference.

As the Lord sends out his sheep among wolves, I know that only by listening to the heart of the father am I able to help the lambs who have been placed in my care, even in the darkest of tunnels. And make no mistake. The tunnel is darkening. But unlike the Tenebrae, the light of Christ will never be extinguished.

So here's to flatbeds, tunnels, light, and stepping into the will of God. Salvation secures a reservation on the flatbed train. God himself will navigate our way through the tunnel. As the engineer, he lights the way. We need only receive and switch on the light.

As permanent passenger on God's railway, we can each take responsibility for seeing that our kids, grandkids, and friends have a ticket. Sharing the good news of the gospel, witnessing to our own testimonies and experience, encourage the generations behind to make reservations on the train. No amount of darkness can extinguish that eternal light.

Full steam ahead! God's flatbed is on the move!

All aboard!

WHAT IS CONCEIVED IN HER

> Joseph son of David, do not be afraid to take Mary as your wife, because what is conceived in her is from the Holy Spirit.
>
> —Matthew 1:20

Today children are born out of wedlock all the time, but in Jesus's day, it was a rare disgrace. Can you imagine Joseph's horror when he discovered that his fiancée, Mary, was pregnant—and not by him? I often wonder what his family said. What did they think?

But the Lord works in mysterious ways. What is conceived by God often can't be comprehended by man. God's ways are not our ways; God's plans are not our plans. How he thought up this one is beyond me. That's why it's called a mystery. Only God himself could conceive of using a humble girl from Nazareth as the bearer of light to the Gentiles, the carrier of the Christ-child.

I often wonder what went through young Mary's mind. How did she come to be the handmaiden of the Lord? According to *Webster's Collegiate Dictionary*, a *handmaiden* is "a personal maid or female servant."[1] Mary most definitely fits this description. As a servant of the Lord, she heard his plans and agreed without even an argument.

Not me! I would have typed a list of questions I wanted answered before I would even consider the question. I suppose that's why God chose Mary and not someone like me.

Joseph, too, was a man of extraordinary faith. It is no accident that the Lord placed the two of them together. The Lord visited him, too, to reassure him regarding his plans.

A close scrutiny shows that God did not give many details (he rarely does), only a general picture of Jesus's purpose on earth. He told Joseph, "You are to give him the name Jesus because he will save his people from their sins" (Matthew 1:21).

Isn't that like the Holy Spirit? He comes to us in ways we don't expect, through dreams, circumstances, visions, and other people. Not only that, but he gives us messages that we don't understand: *Build an ark… March around Jericho seven times… Give him the name Jesus because he will save his people from their sins.*

I love the church calendar, especially the seasons of Advent and Christmas, because they are reminders of God's plan for salvation. Each year, we get to revisit this plan, and each year, we see his truth in a new light, just one more piece of the mystery.

Puzzles are a favorite activity in my family, especially jigsaw puzzles. We keep one going in our cabin in Colorado 24/7. Just a walk-by can bring up that long-lost, much-needed piece that is the key to a whole section.

Advent and Christmas are the keys to the spiritual puzzle.

The word *advent* comes from the Latin word *adventus,* meaning "arrival."[2] In the Christian calendar, it is a time of preparation, a period of expectant waiting. Following close on its heels is Christmas, the celebration of the birth of our Lord and Savior. As we read the Scriptures, we look toward the coming of Christ in a dual way.

The Latin *adventus* is the translation of the Greek word *parousia,* which refers to the time of prayer and fasting before the coming of Christ at the Incarnation. In addition, it also reminds us of the second coming of Christ, a time in the future to which Christians look forward.

I wish he'd come soon, but as a woman of years, I know a lot about waiting. It seems I've been waiting for something all my life—a graduation or marriage, the birth of a grandbaby, the next move, the next phase of life, the next test. Like Tevye, the milkman in *Fiddler on the Roof*, who'd been waiting for the Messiah for almost two thousand years, I guess we can wait a little bit longer for his return.

Surveying the world, I see chaos multiplying exponentially. Fear and confusion are in people's eyes, hopelessness and helplessness in their voices. Darkness and despair are everywhere. Fear has taken hold, and many do not know how to respond. If you travel abroad, you especially see this.

Yet Jesus is clear. He tells us not to be afraid, that he is with us always. "And surely I am with you always, to the very end of the age" (Matthew 28:20).

The question is personal: how do we impart the depth of Mary and Joseph's faith in the midst of a secular world? One of the best times to step out in faith is Christmas—after all, it is Christ's birthday.

When you think of it, a jolly, fat man with a beard dressed in red is pretty farfetched. Yet our world has bought into this image, bringing it to the forefront over the King of kings.

When it comes to Christmas, I'm as much of a child as my grandchildren. I love to give gifts, and decorating the Christmas tree is the highlight of our family get-togethers. But as a grandmother, I also have the opportunity to teach my grandchildren the difference between fact and fantasy. That one man can ride a sleigh around the world in one night delivering toys is a fantasy for childhood. When they get older, better to teach that the Word became flesh, that the Savior of the world came to us as a babe wrapped in swaddling clothes, lying in a manager, and that he is still with us today.

This last Christmas, God did just that in spite of me. He did the talking while I did the walking. This was my Christmas with kids and grandkids, and we experienced our first ever white Christmas in Fort Worth, Texas—a blizzard on Christmas Eve! Overwhelmed by five grandkids, two dogs, an army of adults, twenty-five coming to dinner, and wet towels and wetter floors, I suggested going to the Christmas pageant at 4:00 p.m. hoping to keep my sanity. I had no idea that God would move in such a fantastic way.

Arriving in a flurry of snow and wind, the church leaders greeted us with a question: "Who wants to be in the Christmas pageant?" Three eager little hands were raised as their owners volunteered to go backstage, dress as sheep, and become part of the flock. Without rehearsal, they performed their parts to perfection, and the true story of Christmas was imparted through no effort of my own.

Outside of church, speaking the truth in this environment is a challenge. But speak it we must. There is light at the end of the tunnel in so many areas, if we would just be bold.

As believers, we have the opportunity to walk out our faith in a new way. By sharing our faith, by speaking the truth in love, perhaps we can make an impact in a world that has turned itself upside down.

I have been encouraged that there are more voices on television testifying to God and his presence in the world. Not long ago, *Good Morning America* featured a story about a woman named Angela, the victim of a would-be robber. Turning to prayer, she had a forty-minute conversation with the young man who recanted, put his gun away, and prayed to receive Jesus. Her testimony has confounded many, yet her name, Angela, means "messenger of God." Not only did she bring the gospel to this would-be robber, but she also was God's messenger of love. She certainly more than lived up to her name.

We, too, can be a witness for Christ. We just have to be creative. Perhaps this is the year to simplify our buying at Christmas. Telling our friends and family that we care more about celebrating the season and giving to the less fortunate than to ourselves is a good place to start. Perhaps we could share the Christmas story in a homeless shelter. Buying gifts for a family from the giving tree is a good way to pour out the love of Christ. Sponsoring an African child and sending him or her to school or praying for families affected by natural disasters are great ways to live out the Scripture. Giving, sacrifice, prayer, and salvation are the best gifts we have to give at Christmas.

Like Mary, let's be vessels of the Holy Spirit. Let's carry the Christ child to a hurting world. Maybe, just maybe, our sacrifice and willingness to share will impact others in ways they have not been impacted before.

Do not be afraid, for what is conceived in you is from the Holy Spirit.

CHRIST IN CHRISTMAS

> Do not be afraid. I bring you good news of great joy...
> Today in the town of David a Savior has been born to you;
> he is Christ the Lord.
>
> —Luke 2:10–12

"I bring you good news of great joy..." What an amazing message. Just as relevant today as two thousand years ago, these words have been repeated and received by countless millions. Taken to heart for generations, this declaration of hope has brought light into the darkness and hope to the hopeless. It is the good news of salvation and peace to those separated from God.

Yet billions of people have either not received the Word or have heard but rejected it. Instead, they ignore the birth of our Lord and Savior and choose only to celebrate Santa, who lives at the North Pole, rides a sleigh pulled by reindeer, and brings toys to all the good little boys and girls around the world. What has our world come to?

More often than not, I, too, have included Santa in our Christmas traditions. I wrap presents, visit Santa at malls, hang stockings, leave cookies and milk by the fireplace, and pretty much have participated in and perpetuated this fable my entire adult life. Sadly, there have been times when I have focused on the coming of Saint Nicholas far more than the birth of Jesus Christ.

Shame on me! And shame on the church for not setting the world aright.

Now don't get me wrong. I love Christmas as much as the next person. And I'm not saying that it's necessarily wrong to include Santa in your family's Christmas traditions. But recently, I've been more focused on the Word, aware of the truth of Christmas. A crusader of biblical proportions, I'm determined to keep the record straight about Jesus and what his birth means to me, to my friends and family, and to the world.

But how do I fulfill my mission without ruffling feathers and disrupting routines? How do I stay true to my faith while living in the world? Or, as Jesus describes it, being in the world without being of the world?

Contemplating this dilemma, I designed my own personal "Savvy Grandmother Plan" to put Christ back into Christmas. In just four easy steps, I can focus on the true meaning of Christmas.

Step 1: Be grounded in the Word. Being fully grounded in the Word from Genesis to Revelation helps me understand the message of Christ. By knowing God's plan and articulating it clearly, I am better able to partner with him to further his work on earth.

Step 2: Spread the gospel boldly; speak the truth in love. Being bold in the Christmas season should be a cinch. What better time to share Jesus, especially in the malls and stores, than when the world is celebrating Jesus's birthday? Yes, Christ is with us. Yes, God's love did come down from heaven. Yes, the baby Jesus did grow up into Christ crucified. Yes, he is still among us.

Step 3: Use the symbols of Christmas to tell the Christmas story. When the shepherds guarded their flocks by night, angels came down from heaven to proclaim the good news. As a bright light surrounded them, the heavenly hosts announced the birth to a stunned audience. Today, we are God's heavenly host here on earth, sent to announce the good news. What better way than to use the symbols of the season as a springboard to tell the greatest story ever told?

Step 4: Be intentional; research. Make a list of potential opportunities to share the gospel. Here are just a few ideas that others have shared with me:

- Nativity or Crèche: Created on Christmas Eve 1224, by St. Francis of Assisi, a man who walked after God's own heart. He used real people and animals to tell the story of the first Christmas. Today Nativity scenes and crèches can still be purchased at local department stores. In fact, I collect them from all over the world. As each figure is handled and placed in position, the story comes alive to a child.

- Christmas Tree: Some say the Christmas tree began in the eighth century with St. Boniface and newly baptized Christians who gathered together to renounce paganism. Others say it originated in Germany, where it was decorated with apples and candles. Prince Albert brought it to England and it was later spread to America by the Pilgrims. The vertical stature of the tree points upward, reminding us of God's faithfulness and heavenly home. The green on the leaves represents eternal life. The branches reach out to embrace humanity in love.

- Christmas Carols: St. Francis and others sang the first carols around the crèche. By studying the meaning of and words of some of our favorites—"Hark the Herald Angels Sing," "It Came upon a Midnight Clear," "We Three Kings of Orient Are," "O Come All Ye Faithful"— tell the story for us. We just have to retell it in words and songs that people can understand.

- Jesse Tree: This is a special tree decorated each week of December with ornaments representing Old Testament stories from creation to Christ's birth. Each figure builds on the previous one, giving a child the big picture of God's purpose and plan from the beginning.

- Candy Canes: These are great teaching tools, especially if you eat them as you talk. The cane is the shape of a "J" for Jesus or a shepherd's hook for the shepherd of the sheep. The candy is sweet to remind us that we are fed on the sweetness of the gospel and are given daily manna by god. The hardness of the candy reminds us that Jesus is our rock, our strong tower, our protector.

- Christmas Star: The star of Bethlehem announced Christ's birth. It led the shepherds and the wise men to the manger and reminds us to follow the light of Christ.

- Red and Green: Red symbolizes the blood of Christ. Green reminds us of the hope of things to come, of victory over death.

- Advent Wreath: A family tradition of lighting a candle each week in the four weeks preceding Christmas, the accompanying Scripture readings explain God's plan of salvation from the Old Testament to the cross. Family discussion, singing, and prayer keep the focus on Christ and God's plan of redemption.

Being a storyteller is not hard when we have visual aids to guide us. Be creative, do your research, and find ways to share more than just a surface telling of the Christmas story. By teaching, holding, and loving, we are building memories as we plant seeds of eternal life in the hearts of our precious charges and those in our sphere of influence.

There is no greater gift than the gift of eternal life wrapped in a package of grace. To be the bearer of this great gift is to bestow an eternal heritage upon those we love the most. What better legacy than to prepare a child or friend for the coming of the Christ child, not only on Christmas Eve, but in his or her own heart?

part 5

revisiting history

WE HOLD THESE TRUTHS TO BE SELF-EVIDENT...

It is for freedom that Christ has set us free. Stand firm, then, and do not let yourselves be burdened again by a yoke of slavery.

—Galatians 5:1

I love the Fourth of July and everything about it: hot dogs, parades, fireworks, and apple pie. Images and memories of days gone by bring a smile to my lips and joy to my heart. Memories of friends and family, bicycle parades, watermelon by the swimming pool, homemade ice cream, and watching fireworks over the lake with my kids are memories that I will hold for a lifetime.

I love the way Lake City, Colorado— a small town in the mountains where we go every year—celebrates Independence Day. A true old-fashioned party, from red, white, and blue parades with horses, motorcycles, and classic cars to an old-fashioned picnic in the park with three-legged races and egg tosses, it is Americana at its finest. The whole town participates. One year, we decorated our Jeep and rode in the parade with our grandchildren. We prefer, though, to sit on the sidelines and watch the fire engines pass as we gather the candy thrown by the participants from their floats and autos.

But the Fourth of July is more than a parade. The truth of what we celebrate should bring us to our knees. Meditating on the significance of the day and the sacrifices made should, if not boggle the mind, at least take our breath away.

Men and women, in our homeland and on foreign soil, fought and died to preserve these freedoms at great cost to themselves and their families. They sacrificed so that we might be free. But the truths that seemed self-evident to them do not seem as clear to us two-and-a-half centuries later. It would serve us well to study the reason behind their declaration. By refreshing our memories, we can imprint these truths on our hearts and teach them to our children and grandchildren and the next generation.

On July 4, 1776, one of the greatest documents in human history was signed by John Hancock and fifty-five other patriots. This document was filled with truth. First signed by the delegates to the Continental Congress, it declared our freedom from British rule. Later ratified by the colonies, it became the law of the land. Delegates to the Continental Congress came from all thirteen colonies. Eighteen were merchants, fourteen were farmers, and four were doctors. Twenty-two were lawyers, and nine were judges. One was a clergyman, and one a Roman Catholic. Fifty-two of the fifty-six signers were Christian, and four were former or full-time preachers. Many were the sons of clergy.

The Declaration of Independence, based on Judeo-Christian principles, gives thanks to God as the ruler of the universe. It acknowledges that God has bestowed and endowed certain rights upon all people, drawing from the social philosophies and political justice of John Locke, Thomas Paine, Cicero, Adam Smith, Charles Montesquieu, and the Bible.

The Declaration's founding philosophy is immortalized and engraved on some of our most cherished monuments. Moses, holding the Ten Commandments, is on the outside of the

Supreme Court. "In God We Trust" is inscribed in gold behind the Speaker's rostrum in the House Chamber and on our money. An inscription by John Adams, the first president to inhabit the White House, is cut into the marble facing of the State Dining Room: "I pray heaven to bestow the best of blessings on this house and on all that shall hereafter inhabit it. May not but honest and wise men ever rule under this roof." On the tomb of the Unknown Soldier: "Here rests in honored glory an American soldier known but to God." Upon the capstone of the Washington Monument are the words *Laus Deo*, meaning "Praise God."[1]

Washington D.C. is an amazing treasure trove of history and scripture. When Jack was twelve, we took him on a trip to the Capitol. Our goal was to instill in him the truth regarding the foundation of freedom and the role of God in the founding of our country. Sharing the scriptures etched in stone, visiting Mount Vernon, the home of our first president, visiting the Capitol and the White House, seeing the Jefferson and Lincoln Memorials, visiting Arlington Cemetery, and talking about the men and women who gave their lives for freedom—it doesn't get any better than that.

As teenagers in high school, we memorized the words of the preamble to the Constitution. Tested time and again on their meaning, we spent many a classroom discussion on the impact they have on our world and families today.

> We hold these truths to be self-evident that all me are created equal, that they are endowed by their creator, with certain unalienable Rights, that among these are Life, Liberty, and the pursuit of Happiness.[2]

According the *World Book Encyclopedia*, "The signers of the Declaration believed it was obvious that "all men" were created equal and had rights that could not be taken away. By "all men," they meant people of every race and of both sexes. The right to "life" included the right to defend oneself against physical attack and unjust government. The right to "liberty" meant the right to criticize the government, to worship freely, and to form a government that protects liberty. The "pursuit of happiness" meant the right to own property and to have it safeguarded. It also meant the right to strive for the good of all people, not only for one's personal happiness."[3] In other words, be a servant. Sound familiar?

This is truth.

As Christians, it is our right and privilege to take "these truths" one step further. For they not only have to do with life and liberty, but with the freedom we have in our religion. To worship God openly, without fear of arrest and prosecution, is the greatest freedom on earth.

Truth is an interesting thing. After a certain age, one just senses things. I wonder if this is what the Founding Fathers experienced. Call it age, wisdom, life experience, or intuition—we just know things.

We all have our gifts. When I was a young mom, my gift had to do with money. Not very deep, but that was my gift. To the surprise of my sons, I could guess the total value of all the items in my grocery cart. With no calculator, notes, or price comparison, I was usually within five dollars of the total bill.

"Eighty dollars and twelve cents," I would call out. "One hundred thirty-eight."

With bated breath, they waited to see how close I would come. I don't know how I did it, but I was always close. If I didn't make the five-dollar limit, I had to buy them gum.

Oh the gifts of the young mind. What trivia and folly we hold close to the heart.

In later life, I searched for deeper truth. As a senior, I may not be as adept with figures, but I still have that sense about me. Today my calculations are in the area of truth; my sensors tell me when someone is lying. I don't how it works. Perhaps people reveal themselves with a facial expression or body language. Perhaps it's maturity.

But like the signers of the Declaration of Independence, these truths of God have become self-evident. I can't help but wonder how and why we have become complacent as a nation in our worship and testimony to God. It is one of the questions that confounds and haunts my heart.

As savvy grandmothers, we must pass on these self-evident truths. By pointing them out, by holding them near and dear, others will catch the vision and will be set on fire for God and freedom.

Now these are fireworks worth celebrating!

THE TIMES ARE A-CHANGIN'

> Therefore I tell you, do not worry about your life, what you will eat or drink; or about your body, what you will wear. Is not life more important than food, and the body more important than clothes?
>
> —Matthew 6:25

When I was in my teens and early twenties, I loved Peter, Paul, and Mary—still do.

I remember their songs with fondness, especially since they are still popular today, having survived a fifty-year life span. They were fun, catchy, and easy to learn. A few of my favorites include: *Blowin' In the Wind, Don't Think Twice, Leaving on a Jet Plane, If I Had a Hammer, This Train,* and *500 Miles.*

Some say their songs were social commentaries, maybe even revolutionary, as they spoke of social change and righting wrongs. But as a young girl, that went right over my head. I just dug the music and loved that they loved children. As best I can tell, they included at least one children's song in each album.

Though I might not have agreed with their stance back then, today I'm paying more attention. As the title of one of their songs suggests, the times, they are a'changing. Seems to me this could be a prophetic word for our time, and not in a good way.

As we know, words have meaning. It's important to pay attention to them.

Webster's dictionary defines *revolution* as "a fundamental change in political organization; an activity or movement designed to effect fundamental changes in the socioeconomic situation. [2] Evolution is described as a process of change in a certain direction."

Like it or not, our country is changing. And I don't think for the better.

But is it revolution or evolution? I'm afraid history will be the judge on that one. I'm not willing or probably able to wait for the historical verdict. I want to know now, so I've dedicated myself to an all-out search of facts, specifically concerning American and World history since the 1700s.

A lover of historical fiction, I started by reading and re-reading the authors whose writing and research I trust. I was especially touched by Herman Wouk's *Winds of War* and *War and Remembrance*. His eyes and mine see through the same prism. Written in 1970, the depth of his research and insight astounds me.

As a past history teacher, I recognize that his description is how I remember history. In fact, I taught World and American History right out of college. In my junior and senior classes, all students were required to watch a documentary on the Third Reich which I showed each semester. I later heard Steven Spielberg describe a similar documentary that had a great influence on his making of the movie *Schindler's List*. Perhaps it was the same one. I can't remember the name, but I can remember the horror of it all. It just made one want to understand what happened and why.

The same is true today, so I decided to bone up.

Inspired by recent events, I specifically set about reading of the formation and adoption of the Declaration of Independence and the Constitution. I scoured the basement and attic for my old high school American History teaching notes and textbooks. My search revealed much, and I concluded that textbooks today don't teach the same things I taught or was taught back in the 1960s. There it was, in black and white, the history of our country, slowly being rewritten. Through subtleties, slants, emphasis, omissions, and new themes, our history has morphed over the past fifty years.

By the same token, teaching the truth about our country and the role of God and the Bible is being shifted from the schools to the family. Back in the '50s, when I was in grade school, we opened our day with the Pledge of Allegiance and real prayer to God and Jesus.

Homeschooling was unheard of. We didn't need it. Now I'm not so sure. In some cases, homeschooling does seem to be a good option. Recently, I met an amazing lady at a women's conference, Sally Clarkson. Sally is an author, speaker, and mother of four who promotes the advantages of home schooling. Her book *The Mission of Motherhood* makes a lot of sense.[3]

Surely it's never too late to fill in the blanks left by public education. As grandparents, we can talk to our grandkids about the issues of the day. Who better to teach them critical thinking, debating techniques, and analytical thought? Modeling discernment is the best way I know to teach them to think for themselves.

I once attended a conference where I met a young mom who homeschools her kids. Twice a week, her mother, the grandmother, comes to her house to teach quilting to her boys, ages seven and eight. I was surprised, so I asked what they were quilting. "Quilts on the Civil and Revolutionary War," she replied.

What a wise grandmother. Though I suspect she did most of the quilting and her grandsons did most of the listening, she used her gifts and talents not only to teach history but to make memories. I imagine they will never forget listening to the stories of a grandmother as her fingers sewed the patches of history into a memory quilt made especially for them.

As a child, there was no shortage of political discussion in my home. Politics and the daily news were discussed every night— some nights a little more loudly than others. In the process, we learned to think and form opinions. We learned how to debate and back up our positions with fact. We might not agree but we all knew where everyone stood.

Today, whether in the political or spiritual realm, my opinion is rarely in question. Lucky for me God gave me sons to push me to the next level. Recently one challenged me to compare news stories from opposing media outlets. For three weeks, I checked the websites of eight different outlets: four liberal, four conservative. I even charted their differences for my own information. The exercise not only solidified my own position, but it also gave me clear talking points and a platform from which to debate.

A most interesting discussion transpired. As I shared my observations, I also talked about my experience of prayer in school growing up. I quickly realized this world was totally foreign to him.

"But Mom, you attended a parochial school," he responded.

"Not so," I replied. "This was not a church school. This was a public school. Religion and prayer were not only in the public schools, they were also at the sporting events, graduation exercises, and more. We sang 'Fairest Lord Jesus' and 'God of our Fathers' at my sixth-grade Thanksgiving program. There were no conflicting messages. Everywhere—church, school, and home— children got the same message."

"But what about the separation of church and state?" he asked.

It hit me in the face. My son had no frame of reference for the world I grew up in. The change had been so dramatic that his generation had no idea what it used to be like. How could I have let this happen?

As often happens with God, this topic came up again not long afterward with one of my grandkids. But this time, this savvy grandmother was prepared. When Jack reported that he was getting out of school on December 22 for winter break and could come visit me, I took advantage of the teachable moment.

I carefully instructed from the other end of the phone: "You mean *Christmas break*."

"No, Marme, it's winter break," he said.

Raising myself up to all of my five-foot-six-inches, I told him that indeed it was Christmas break. That Christ was born, that the son of God was made man and came to earth, and that is why the celebration began in the first place. Christmas started out as a religious holiday, and that is what it still is.

"The school can call it anything it wants," I said in a firm voice, "but it's Christmas break, and that's what I'm calling it."

No budging for this savvy grandmother.

The Scripture tells us not to worry about what we will eat or drink (Matthew 6:25). But I do worry for my grandchildren. Will they drink the Kool-Aid of secular humanism, or will they drink the pure, nourishing milk of the Word of God?

Truly there is a cancer in our country. When you take God out of the schools and the public arena, you wind up with revolution-ized mores, unethical behavior, political correctness, and anarchy. And that can't be good for anyone.

Evolution or revolution, you decide. But standing up for what one believes is not a matter of age, political correctness, or prin-ciple; it's what a savvy grandmother does.

Peter, Paul and Mary may credit blowing in the wind as the answer to these issues. I have to say I agree. But in my book that means God. He's everywhere and he is blowing in the wind.

BOOTS WERE MADE FOR WALKING

A man is a slave to whatever has mastered him.

—2 Peter 2:19

I love boots. Never without, there are so many different kinds for many different occasions: cowboy boots, hiking boots, rain boots, army boots, firemen boots, combat boots, marching boots, riding boots, and baby boots—something for everyone.

When Strother was three, he loved boots, too. Still does. Recently, he wore a pair of cowboy boots that were too big for him, hand-me-downs from his cousin, Jack, to his cousin, James, and now to him. He adores them and wears them everywhere. Eventually he'll outgrow them and pass them down to Hodge. No matter that they have had to be resoled a number of times; they still work well.

Seeing Strother and how his resoled boots work for him, I couldn't help but reflect on the many boots of our history and what they've meant to the soul of our nation. Though they've been tested and resoled again and again, they've worked pretty well for us.

America's boots have marched to the fife and drum many times over, from freedom, life, liberty, inalienable rights, and equality to the pursuit of happiness. Wars have been fought and books written to preserve these freedoms.

With God as our foundation, and the Constitution to ground us, taking a look at a few of the boots that have marched and held us to a standard of freedom might be a good idea. As we all know, history repeats itself. If we don't learn from the mistakes of the past, we are destined to repeat them.

First, there were the boots of the Continental Congress: men who came to Philadelphia to forge a new country. Bringing a belief in life, liberty, and the pursuit of happiness, these men knew their Creator and were willing to stand on his principals when forging a new government. Students of history themselves, they read the great philosophers such as Cicero, Thomas Paine, and John Locke, men who were willing to risk everything—freedom for principles.

Then there were the boots of the Revolutionary War: men who battled weather and poor conditions, lack of sleep, and scarcity of food, in order to fight for freedom. These dedicated soldiers, marched through mud, rain, sleet, and snow in the worst of conditions. Some even lost their physical boots in the process. But all were willing to sacrifice their lives in order to separate us from a tyrannical king—freedom from tyranny.

Beginning to sound familiar? Freedom…kings…dictators…control…sacrifice…

In 1860, our country wore the boots of the Civil War. During this five-year, bloody conflict, slavery and freedom were on the line. Families were torn apart, a nation in tatters until a godly man was raised up to lead our nation in equality—freedom from slavery.

Next were the boots of World War I. Flamed by nationalism, military alliances, and secret diplomacy, these boots were the boots to end all war. With the development of the tank, hand grenade, submarine, airplane, and automatic weapons, the men who wore these boots suffered through modern warfare, the likes of which have escalated into weapons of mass destruction. And now their unintended consequences threaten the very existence of our world today. These boots could have changed the world for freedom, but they didn't—freedom for democracy.

Soon thereafter came World War II. Nations joined together against the forces of evil to fight for the freedom of nations. Countries invaded and occupied by despots relied on American boots, which freed the world, especially Europe, from tyranny and genocide. With God as our standard, morality and integrity reached across the ocean to save the world. Dictatorships, Nazism, and Fascism threatened on every side. These boots brought liberation—freedom from tyranny and evil dictatorships.

The 1960s brought the boots of the civil rights movement. The voice of reason and fairness, Martin Luther King Jr., Rosa Parks, and others brought the inequality of civil rights to the forefront. With courage and steadfastness, they marched forward wearing civil rights boots as they gained freedom for the oppressed—freedom from prejudice.

Most recently are the boots of Iraq, Afghanistan, and the Persian Gulf Wars, soldiers willing to fight on foreign soil to give freedom to others. This enemy, the most dangerous of all, is a satanic force that cannot be seen or known but which threatens the very essence of life—freedom from terrorism.

Military boots have been responsible for freedom in this country for many years. These men and women not only have soul, but they have courage and integrity, willingness, and compassion. They wear boots so big we'll never be able to fill them on our own.

The boots worn in domestic and foreign conflicts over the last 250 years have kept us free. America has done her job. Never in the history of the world has a country given so much to so many in aid, food, medicine, and inventions. Founded as a Christian nation, the light of Christ has been sent to pour out on those less fortunate. Sure, we've made mistakes, but never before have so many flocked to these borders, seeking a new life and an opportunity to succeed. As a result, they have received the spiritual and material blessings that have made us strong. Today they live under the same protection, the same freedoms of speech, press, and religion as we do.

My housekeeper has worked for me for twenty-five years. She came to this country not as a citizen and not speaking English. Over time, she has learned our language, become a citizen, built a beautiful life for her four children, and is now proud to be sending her firstborn to college. Anna's birthday is July 4, the same day she got her citizenship. On that day, she says she has a double blessing— her physical birth and her physical and spiritual freedom. Anna inspires me to be more than I am.

As I've aged, I've developed a hunger to learn more about my country's roots. As a teacher of history, I know my grandkids are not learning what I did. I want and need to know more. I want to get it right. Who better than my generation to research and pass on the correct history to the next generation? We certainly have the passion, energy, and time.

One of my recent new year's resolutions has been to collect credible books on history written before the 1960's. When Jim's parents died and my mom moved, I inherited an extensive collection which I am putting together as a legacy for my children and grandchildren.

Perhaps I'm in process of returning to my roots. But I'm convinced that only by learning history will our country avoid the mistakes of the past. Do we really understand the courageous sacrifices of our ancestors? Are we aware of the generosity of our nation corporately, as well as individually, during times of disaster? Do we really know about the people who sacrificed so that we could wear the boots of comfort and prosperity today?

A popular song back in my teaching days was "These Boots Were Made for Walking." Some of you may remember it. Cute, perky Nancy Sinatra sang her heart out in white boots and a miniskirt. I have unashamedly hijacked the title, taking the liberty to reappoint its meaning. Rather than taking revenge against something, my boots are made for walking toward something, standing up for what is right and good in our country.

That's what boots did in our history. That's what American boots do today. As grandmothers and patriots, we have the ability to put on our grandmother boots, learn our history, memorize it, and pass it on.

We have big boots to fill. We may not be fighting men and women on the battlefield, but we are warriors of truth in the minefields. By studying God's role in our history, we will be better prepared to pass down the foundation of our country to those who come behind.

The spirit of freedom that has walked for over two hundred years in our country and over two thousand years in the Bible continues to ring. Let's put on our freedom boots so that the soul of our country can survive.

TEN SENIORS WHO CHANGED THE WORLD

> Therefore, since we are surrounded by such a great cloud
> of witnesses, let us throw off everything that hinders…and
> let us run with perseverance the race marked out for us.
>
> —Hebrews 12:1

If my calculations are correct, a number of the books of the Bible
were written by seniors in their golden years.

Today culture demands retirement or cutting back work hours
by a certain age. Not so the disciples. They worked until they
died or were martyred. Not a good retirement plan, but definitely
a kingdom-building opportunity.

As best I can tell, if the disciples were around thirty years of
age when Jesus died, this is how it would stack out. Matthew and
Luke would have written their gospels between fifty and sixty
years of age, John between sixty and seventy, James forty-nine to
fifty-nine, Peter fifty-two to sixty-two. Add Moses, who wrote
the Pentateuch, somewhere between seventy-six and one hundred and sixteen, as well as Isaiah, sixty to seventy-nine, Daniel
sixty-nine plus, Jeremiah about seventy-nine, and Zechariah
twenty to sixty. This is a formidable group indeed. And don't
forget Abraham was fifty when God called him out of Ur of the
Chaldeas and one hundred when he fathered Isaac.[1]

Think about it. These great men of God all began their writing careers as they approached Medicare and Social Security age. Now, I'm no mathematician, but even the roughest calculations surmise that these men were not spring chickens when they penned the Scripture. Perhaps it was their life experience that made the difference, maybe their observation of humanity. More than likely, it was their walk of faith, obedience, and the anointing of the Holy Spirit. But whatever it was, clearly, they did their best work in their senior years.

God likes seniors. He likes them a lot. Although this is not a scientific study, some conclusions can be reached. First, the Lord expects much as we approach the golden years. But more importantly, our most prolific spiritual years lie ahead.

Again, numbers are not my thing, but it appears that as these men aged, they became more dedicated, more sold out for the Lord. They were willing to sacrifice everything, to take up their crosses and follow him, literally and physically. Most wrote their books between the ages of forty and eighty. With each year, they allowed the Lord to grow their faith.

History is full of other examples of seniors living out their faith. In her book *The Hiding Place,* Corrie ten Boom tells how she and her sister, Betsy, at the age of fifty, ran the largest underground resistance network in Holland during World War II.[2] God gave them everything they needed for the journey and more. So, too, will he give to us — no matter our age.

David Wilkerson, the author of *The Cross and The Switchblade,*[3] was in his fifties when the Holy Spirit called him back to New York City to found the Times Square Church. He had lived there in the 1950s and '60s, when he ministered to drug addicts, gang members, and inner-city kids. He left for a season but returned to pastor that church for more than thirty years.

The average age of the fifty-six signers of the Declaration of Independence was forty-five. Benjamin Franklin was seventy, Samuel Adams, fifty-four, and John Witherspoon, the only clergyman, fifty-three. Not to be outdone, George Washington was sixty-seven when he became our first president in 1789. Clearly, God uses seniors as voices of reason and wisdom.

These historical figures have written their words and opinions clearly for us to read. So, too, have our spiritual patriarchs. Testimonies of experience, observations, recordings, and words of wisdom abound. Holy Spirit-inspired, these men were not afraid to lay it on the line. Filled with conviction and the Holy Spirit, they could not be disobedient.

So grandmothers, what are we waiting for? Our most productive season is ahead.

Who knows what lives we will affect? As savvy grandmothers, we may not all be writers, but we all have gifts and talents. God leaves nothing to chance. Artists, singers, painters, scrap bookers, quilters, cooks, gardeners, all gifts and talents apportioned to glorify the Lord in ways that only we can.

Over the next few years, let's determine how radical we can be in our faith. How far are we willing to go to proclaim the goodness of God? What part will we have in ushering in the kingdom?

God calls everyone to use their gifts and talents. Recently, a boldness has emerged in the media as commentators, columnists, and opinion-makers reveal their faith on radio and TV. Paul Harvey, on his popular radio program *The Rest of the Story*, was unabashedly open about his faith on a number of occasions. Tim Tebow, University of Florida quarterback, uses a football stadium as his pulpit to glorify the Lord.

Radical or no, faith changes the world. Perhaps God is whispering something in your ear at this very moment—something he has been preparing in you for a long time; perhaps something you have been in training for and didn't even know it. The word of the day is *persevere*. As the Scripture says, let us all run the race for which we have been appointed (Hebrews 12:1).

Although we aren't as fast as we used to be, even we seniors have something to add to the race. If we can't jog, surely we can stroll. For the best is yet to come. And that is no calculation.

THE EAGLE
HAS LANDED

But those who hope in the Lord will renew their strength.
They will soar on wings like eagles; they will run and not
grow weary, they will walk and not be faint.

—Isaiah 40:31

Everyone remembers where they were during the assassination of John F. Kennedy and 9/11. So, too, do we remember where we were in 1969 when *Apollo 11* landed on the moon.

I was in Galveston, Texas, five months pregnant. Jim and I watched the landing in our two-room apartment on an old black-and-white TV that had been his parents' and was now ours. Looking like something out of *Star Wars*, it lived on a bookshelf made of green-painted cinder blocks and wood-stained shelves.

A hide-a-bed sofa completed the décor and was a stroke of genius, since the landing was at 9:56 CST. Since no one had TVs in their bedrooms, sleeping on the hide-a-bed allowed us to not miss a moment of this history-making event. With just a click of the on button, the moon's surface came into focus. Of course, there were no remotes in those days, so we had to get off the sofa to turn the TV on, a minor inconvenience in the scheme of things.

We watched in awe as the lunar module landed. We heard with our own ears, in real time, Neil Armstrong's now-famous words, "Houston, Tranquility Base here. The Eagle has landed."

America had recaptured the space race.

Today, the Hubble telescope takes thousands of pictures from space—but back then, seeing the heavenlies for the first time was truly a spiritual experience. After the mission, the pictures printed in *Time* and *Life* magazines showed a heaven that heretofore had been beyond our imagination.

As Neil Armstrong prepared to step onto the moon's surface, Buzz Aldrin, orbiting miles above the moon's surface, asked the viewing audience for a moment of silence. He then privately took Communion and spent time with God in prayer, surely praying protection and provision over his two comrades. His moment of silence was private because he was forbidden to share his faith by law following an incident on the *Apollo 8* mission six months before.

It was the first time in my memory that a public figure was muzzled in regard to his faith.

Six months earlier, on December 24, 1968, the erosion of freedom of speech and religion infected the public domain. On that day, three astronauts aboard the *Apollo 8*—William Anders, James Lovell, and Frank Borman—testified to the Lord and his creation of the world. As their spacecraft orbited the moon, they read from Genesis. The visual movement from dark to light on the moon's surface, the sun's rising through the spacecraft's window, dramatically accompanied their words.

It was a spiritual moment for even the most skeptical:

William Anders:

"We are now approaching lunar sunrise, and for all the people back on Earth, the crew of Apollo 8 has a message that we would like to send to you. In the beginning God created the heaven and the earth. And the earth was without form, and void; and darkness was upon the face of the deep. And the Spirit of God moved upon the face of the waters. And God said, Let there be light: and there was light. And God saw the light, that it was good: and God divided the light from the darkness."

James Lovell:

"And God called the light Day, and the darkness he called Night. And the evening and the morning were the first day. And God said, Let there be a firmament in the midst of the waters, and let it divide the waters from the waters. And God made the firmament, and divided the waters which were under the firmament from the waters which were above the firmament: and it was so. And God called the firmament heaven. And the evening and the morning were the second day."

Frank Borman:

"And God said, Let the waters under the heavens be gathered together unto one place, and let the dry land appear: and it was so. And God called the dry land Earth; and the gathering together of the waters he called Seas: and God saw that it was good."

Borman then added, "And from the crew of Apollo 8, we close with good night, good luck, a Merry Christmas—and God bless all of you—all of you on the good Earth." 1

As a result of that reading, a destructive evil was set into motion: Madalyn Murray O'Hair initiated a lawsuit against the US government, alleging violations of the First Amendment.

Today, some forty years later, I'm a grandmother. I couldn't see what was happening then with the erosion of our First Amendment: "Congress shall make no law respecting an establishment of religion, or prohibiting the free exercise thereof..."[1] But today I see. And I'm appalled.

Buzz Aldrin's description of the lunar surface and the name of his book, *Magnificent Desolation*, is a perfect metaphor for what is happening in our world today.[3] This magnificent land that the Spirit hovered over, moved, and breathed upon in Genesis is moving into desolation if we don't stop it.

Astronauts who were bold and brave spoke out then and continue to speak out now. As savvy grandmothers, we, too, should not be afraid to speak out. Let's take control and land this spacecraft of faith, taking our world back for Christ.

As Neil Armstrong, the first human to put his foot on the surface of the moon, said, "That's one small step for man, one giant leap for mankind."[4] Although his words crackled through an imperfect transmitter made by man, he experienced a perfect heavenly body made by God.

These facts are not something your kids will read in a history book.

As savvy grandmothers and women of all ages, it is time to teach history to our children and the world. Let's rediscover and testify to God's role in the creation of the universe, our country, and our constitution. Let us tell the faith stories of the brave men and women who have ventured out and died to preserve our freedoms.

DO THE RIGHT THING

> After desire has conceived, it gives birth to sin; and sin, when it is full-grown, gives birth to death.
>
> —James 1:15

Governor Mike Huckabee was recently on TV promoting his book, *Do the Right Thing*.[1] As best I can tell, the title pretty much says it all.

"Do the right thing" is part of my own personal philosophy. When I was a young child, my stepfather, Guppy, always told me to "do the right thing." I was lucky enough to have him around to guide and mentor me as to exactly what the right thing was. Whenever I got confused, I could ask him and trust that he knew best.

But what happens when I'm the parent or grandparent? What is the right thing then? Where do I go to determine the right thing, especially in tough and challenging times?

The Bible, of course, is our foremost reference, but there are many worthwhile documents and organizations that promote good moral and ethical behavior. Many secular organizations, as well as men and books in our history, espouse biblical principles and applications, and some don't even know that they came from the mouth of the Lord himself.

Abraham Lincoln, one of the greatest presidents in US history, based his two basic tenets for fighting the Civil War on the Bible and the Declaration of Independence. Accepting the Republican nomination for Senate in 1958, Lincoln delivered this line among others in his most famous speech: "A house divided against itself cannot stand." This quote is directly from the Bible (Mark 3:25) and influenced his determination and resolve to preserve the Union.

The Emancipation Proclamation and the succeeding Thirteenth Amendment, which abolished slavery, shifted Lincoln's emphasis to the Declaration of Independence as the foundation for American political values. His famous Gettysburg Address, delivered in less than two minutes at a Soldiers' National Cemetery dedication, sums up his justification for the war:

> Four score and seven years ago our fathers brought forth on this continent, a new nation, conceived in Liberty, and dedicated to the proposition that all men are created equal. Now we are engaged in a great civil war, testing whether that nation, or any nation so conceived and so dedicated can long endure...We have come to dedicate...a final resting place for those who here gave their lives that that nation might live. It is altogether fitting and proper that we should do this...we cannot dedicate—we cannot consecrate—we cannot hallow—this ground. The brave men, living and dead, who struggled here, have consecrated it, far above our poor power to add or detract...that we here highly resolve that these dead shall not have died in vain—that this nation, under God, shall have a new birth of freedom—and that government of the people, by the people, for the people, shall not perish from the earth.[2]

Abraham Lincoln did the right thing.

So did George Washington. His Farewell Address, written to the people in September 1776, toward the end of his second term as president, is filled with godly and biblical principles as he warns the citizens directly.

Observe good faith and justice towards all nations, culti-
vate peace and harmony with all. Religion and morality
enjoin this conduct; and can it be, that good policy
does not equally enjoin it. It will be worthy of a free,
enlightened, and at no distant period, a great nation,
to give to mankind the magnanimous and too novel
example of a people always guided by an exalted justice and benevolence. Who can doubt that, in the
course of time and things, the fruits of such a plan
would richly repay any temporary advantages which
might be lost by steady adherence to it? Can it be
that Providence has not connected permanent felicity
of a nation with its virtue? The experiment, at least,
is recommended by every sentiment which ennobles
human nature.

Another example is George Marshall, who was the architect
of the Marshall Plan, a recovery plan for Europe following
the destruction of World War II. Secretary of State Marshall
unveiled the plan on the steps of Memorial Church in Harvard
Yard. Whether intentional or unintentional, the rationale for the
US to do whatever necessary to return normal economic growth
to the world was biblical in nature. In 1953, Marshall received
the Nobel Peace Prize on behalf of the American people for his
part in its implementation and success.

I find it intriguing that George Marshall was a distant relative
of former chief justice John Marshall, who was a friend and biog-
rapher to George Washington. Justice Marshall was the longest-
serving chief justice in Supreme Court history. His dedication to
the rule of law and sense of fair play made him a respected and
creative force in guiding our nation in those early years. I like to
think that this generational tie supports the biblical thesis that
the acorn doesn't fall far from the tree, that generational healing

or blessing is passed down in families from one generation to the next (Psalm 78:5–7).

In the breadth of time and in the season appointed, all these men did the right thing.

Last but not least is Alcoholics Anonymous, by far the most comprehensive and successful program for dealing with alcoholism. Founded in 1935 by an Episcopal priest and a layperson, this twelve-step program is based on principles from the book of James. Through a series of twelve steps, members are encouraged to take an honest look at their lives, recognize their failings, become accountable for their transgressions, ask and receive forgiveness, make amends to the offended, and live a faith-filled life. Sounds like doing the right thing to me.

By pondering the book of James, we, too, can develop our own spiritual plan and do the right thing. At the same time, we might just pass along a generational heritage of our own.

If it were New Year's Eve, I would make a list of Savvy Grandmother's New Year's resolutions. So let's pretend. Based on the book of James, let's start with a new beginning.

1. Ask God for wisdom (James 1:5): Remember I can do nothing in my own strength.

2. Persevere in times of trial (James 1:12): Take one day at a time.

3. Be aware of our own evil desires (James 1:14): Take responsibility for oneself.

4. Listen to the Word and do what it says (James 2:14): Walk the talk.

5. Keep a tight rein on the tongue (James 3:5): Words spoken can't be taken back.

6. Ask for forgiveness when wrong (James 3:14): Be accountable when at fault.

7. Love your neighbor as yourself (James 2:12): Do unto others.

8. Be humble of heart (James 3:13): Pride comes before a fall.

9. Tame the tongue (James 3:3): Put a guard over the mouth if necessary.

10. Draw near to God and he will draw near to you (James 4:8): Stay in the Word.

11. Be patient and stand firm (James 5:8): Stay the course.

12. Have patience in the face of suffering (James 5:10): Know this too shall pass.

13. Confess your sins to one another (James 5:16): Confess and be accountable to others.

14. Pray for one another (James 5:16): Walk with others without judgment.

15. Speak the truth in love (James 5:19): Speak the truth without judgment.

Whether we are willing to carry out this agenda is between us and God. Only through his Spirit can God make it happen. But if we daily examine our lives and confess where we fall short, we are farther along in the journey to "doing the right thing" than we were the day before.

Grandmothers have the opportunity to do the right thing in the time we have left, and I'm pretty sure our families will appreciate it.

part 6

revisiting spiritual truth

A STOREHOUSE OF SEEDS

Now he who supplies seed to the sower and bread for food will also supply and increase your store of seed and will enlarge the harvest of your righteousness.

—2 Corinthians 9:10

As far as I'm concerned, calendars should run from September to September, not January to January. Everyone knows that activities of any import start in September and end in May.

The first day of the year in our family is September 1, the opening day of dove season. At that time we gather for fellowship, laughter, cooking, being together, and yes, some hunting. I, myself, am not able to tell the difference between a dove and a quail, but apparently everyone else can, for they get their limit each day with no trouble at all.

My experience with dove and quail is limited to the Old Testament and the dinner table. The dinner table is pretty obvious, but the Scriptures are where I really learn the lessons.

Researching the Bible, I discovered that both dove and quail are signs of the Lord's love and mercy. In the book of Exodus, when the Israelites complained of hunger in the desert, the Lord sent quail for their good pleasure. In the New Testament, he sent the dove as a sign of peace and anointing for the ministry and call of his own son.

Imagine you were an Israelite wandering in the desert. What an exciting time that must have been, birds everywhere, falling from the sky, more than enough to fill the best of dinner tables.

Wouldn't it be nice if that were the way it happened today—birds flying everywhere, everyone eating to their heart's content? And not one shot being fired—a grandmother's dream.

The Lord gave a metaphor to the Israelites of a new beginning with the coming of the quail, a time of dependence and faith in the Lord. By the same token, the dove represents peace for all, Jews and Gentile—a new beginning in the calendar year and in the world.

September is also a new beginning, because fall is the time of the first fruits. After the sowing and planting, the harvest is a visual reminder of the multiplication of the seeds that were planted in the spring. When the first fruits appear, they are gleaned, gathered, and brought unto the altar of the Lord in thanksgiving for his many blessings.

Therefore, first fruits are a reflection and thanksgiving for all the Lord has done. Thinking, reflecting, gathering, and counting, we store our blessings on the altar of his sacrifice and in the vessels of our hearts. Filled with gratitude, we are in a better position to share these blessings with others.

As a grandmother, I am not as concerned with the beginning of the calendar year as I once was. But I am concerned with the harvesting of the seeds, the first fruits.

As I gather what the Lord has been about, I like to set aside those seeds that are the by-product of last year's planting. Finding new ways to interact in God's world, I gather the unexpected seed. As I water and nurture the crops that are the result of this year's harvest, my service continues.

I've always wanted to plant a garden, especially with my grandchildren. The oldest three have lived too far away to do that. But

Jack plants one every year with his mother. He reports they grow lettuce, tomatoes, cantaloupe, and watermelon. I've never seen any evidence, but I'm told they've been planted.

I'm already making a plan.

This year, I planted my first ever garden in Rule, Texas, once my husband's home, now ours with his parents' passing. Lily, Strother and James did some of the planting while there on a visit. But unfortunately they missed the harvest. My biggest crop was potatoes and onions. Only Strother got to harvest and he loved it. He ran around shouting, "Look at this one, Marme. This one is huge."

He couldn't wait to see the okra, squash, black-eyed peas, carrots, tomatoes, and green beans. Unfortunately he never got back to gather them in their fullness. Not bad for a first-time effort though. Next year I plan to take all my grandchildren to plant and reap in hopes that we'll walk side by side gathering the fruits of the harvest

Not only am I planning a garden, but I'm also preparing to teach my grandkids to nurture and care for the seeds that are sown. Teaching them about first fruits is what I am all about.

Last year, I bought more seeds than I needed, so I put the unused seeds in the freezer. By adding seeds from the harvest to my stash, I can give my grandchildren a real, live "show-and-tell" of sowing, gardening, and first fruits in a language they can understand.

As servants of the living God, we are instructed to offer the biggest and the best of the year's harvest. I want to pass down that picture of offering the first fruits as a representation of the whole harvest.

The Lord's biggest work in my life has been the publication of *Generation G* and now *The Savvy Grandmother*. These books represent the heart of my heart, the seed of my labor. After watching, watering, and nurturing, it's now time to plan next year's crop. I have an idea for a book offering I want to make to the

Lord, but how that will look, I don't know. I do know that the Lord is using the seeds planted to his good purpose.

Part of sacrifice has to do with giving up expectations. By allowing God to use me with those he puts in my path, I can be about his work. Experience has shown me that God is raising up a large group of women writers. As keepers of the faith, they have sown, gathered, and reaped. I can't wait to see the harvest field of fruit they will gather to fill God's storehouses.

On my journey I met Gwen, who had a spiritual experience as she worked with a young girl who was blind from birth. She wants to write this story for future generations. Wendy, a friend I met at a writer's conference, has written a story of healing from abuse. With hard work and effort, she now has a published book entitled *The Jonah's Chronicles*.[4] Sally, a friend in my writer's group, is writing her memoirs in hopes that her journey will encourage other women. Helen, a woman I met at an Easter Seals luncheon, has been harboring an idea for a book for a number of years. With encouragement and support from other writers, hopefully she will find the courage to begin the process.

God is indeed on the move. From every walk of life, women are gathering their stories as a legacy for the next generation. These women are sowing seeds, collecting the first fruits, bearing witnesses to God's mercy. Their testimonies come in every shape and size, as numerous and colorful as the vegetables in my garden.

So what are your stories? Where are they stored? Are you telling them to others? Are you securing them for the next generation?

By being obedient, the first fruits of our labor will become the first fruits of his righteousness. For God alone opens doors; he alone provides opportunity. A worldly harvest promotes worldly gain. Only a harvest of righteousness will do. As savvy grandmothers, we are to walk side by side with the Lord, harvesting his produce.

What more fertile ground than that of friends and family? There are seeds and first fruits everywhere, just waiting the creative hand of a savvy grandmother. As weavers, singers, missionaries, writers, teachers, and evangelists, we grandmothers have the opportunity to reap a mighty harvest by proclaiming the gospel in our own way. Using our gifts and talents as artists, photographers, scrap bookers, harpists, musicians, songwriters, poets, seamstresses, and teachers, we not only leave a legacy for the next generation, we leave our stories of faith to be viewed by countless others, more than we could ever dream or imagine.

The storehouses are full. Let's not wait until the beginning of the new year to gather our first fruits and store them for future generations. Let's start now.

WHO SAYS A MORAL COMPASS IS FOR THE BIRDS?

> All Scripture is God-breathed and is useful for teaching, rebuking, correcting and training in righteousness, so that the man of God may be thoroughly equipped for every good work.
>
> —2 Timothy 3:16–17

A compass is a useful item. Ships use them for navigation. Hikers use them for positioning. Explorers keep them as directional headings. But with all of our technology today, do we really need a compass to tell us where to go?

Yes, today more than ever, we need to pack our compasses when we leave home.

On our tour of the Hudson River Valley, Jim and I learned a lesson about the need for a compass. No artist could capture the vibrancy and colors of the fall foliage as revealed in God's palette. But finding our way through the winding roads was a different story.

Luckily, we took our Garmin with us. A small GPS, this gadget held our future and well-being in its motherboard. Perfectly choreographed for latitude and longitude, it not only gave us a visual but also an audible description of where we were at all times. It quickly became our best friend as we relied on it for every turn.

One of the things I love best about the Garmin is the soft, sweet voice that breaks into the silence when you make a wrong turn. "Recalculating …. Recalculating" the gentle voice nudges.

But not only do we need a *physical* compass, but we also need a *moral* compass to keep our feet grounded. Periodically, based on principle, we need to re*calibrate*. With so many self-proclaimed philosophers, prophets, teachers, and leaders, what is a person to do? Bombarded with opposing codes, contradictory messages, and self-reliant leaders, we don't know whether we should follow the leader, lead the follower, rebel against the bystander, or just hide in a cave.

Now, isn't that what God does for us? In a soft, gentle voice, he continually reminds us that we need to make a change. *Recalibrating,* he whispers. *Recalibrating.*

Recalibrate…recalibrate, that still, small voice whispers in our ear.

But cars are not the only things that require specific directions. Boats, too, are in need of directional technology to guide their way.

Don and Caro are my friends who sailed the inner coastal waterway from the Gulf of Mexico to the St. Lawrence River. One of the things they needed most was a compass. Learning to read and follow its guidance was a major challenge. Courses had to be taken and tests passed in order to navigate the ocean. A compass was a necessity for uncharted waters, especially for storms in the dark of night, a potential life saver that one would not leave home without.

God is no dummy. He knows that deep inside each of us there is an Ichabod Crane, scared, alone on a dark road, afraid of the dark. At any moment, we might encounter a headless horseman galloping in the night. That's why he gave his inspired Word to set us in the right direction, to help us calibrate and recalculate against the unseen enemy.

Think about it—the Bible is sixty-six books written by approximately forty men over fifteen hundred years, with one continuous theme. What are the odds? It boggles the mind. Paul tells us that the Bible was God-breathed (2 Timothy 3:16). Man was just the instrument. From tentmaker to shepherd, fisherman to tax-collector, God used those who were willing and obedient. Different voices, same message. Amazingly, without benefit of a handbook or Xerox machine, these men proclaimed the same message: there is one true God; there is one way to salvation. It would serve us well to heed their tome.

We know that the Bible is a book of wisdom and truth. It is there for the asking. But we must not be headless on this one. Applying biblical principles challenges even the most ardent follower. If we need a code for family values, the Bible is our answer. It guides us in the areas of healthy relationships and unfriendly neighbors, good Samaritans and bad leaders, prodigal sons and forgiving fathers, lost sheep and faithful shepherds. It also offers principles for financial management, marital relationships, parenting skills, and fairness in business practices. It inspires us to reverence for God, his people, and his creation.

On the same trip to the Hudson Valley, Jim and I visited Sleepy Hollow and Sunnyside, the house where Washington Irving wrote of Ichabod Crane in *The Legend of Sleepy Hollow.* We did not see a headless horseman, but we learned the importance of the Hudson River in the settlement of the colonies. Serving as a waterway and a means of transportation, it was used for troop deployment and food transportation during Revolutionary times. Its centrality guided the settlement of our nation, not unlike the Bible, which guides the settlement of our hearts. Navigated by the guts and glory of ancestors, we are the beneficiaries of those early years both physically and spiritually.

Today boats navigate with state-of-the-art technology. But I had no idea how extensive it was until our trip to Alaska. Following our being stranded at the fishing camp we were invited to meet the captain and tour the bridge of the *Voyager*. This was an offer we couldn't refuse.

On the bridge, we observed the technology that transformed the wooden vessel of yesteryear into the steel machine of the twenty-first century. The bridge, as it is known in seafaring circles, is a tightly constructed, high-tech cabin that resembles a large airplane cockpit. Radar, sonar, and solar were packed into the sleekly designed and carefully planned cabin. The *Voyager* incorporated every advantage known to man. Equipped with modern-day navigational systems, it was all-systems-go, full steam ahead.

But what about a world that, if it has a navigational system, does not keep it in tip-top shape?

Recently there have been a series of incidents in the news of teenage bullying and fighting: Young men with two by fours plummeting one another; young girls ganging up on one of their own with verbal blows and hard-thrown fists. In all of these cases, onlookers pass by without stopping. Where are the good Samaritans? Why does no one stop to render aid?

In the Scripture, the story of the Good Samaritan, the priests, Levites, and teachers of the law were out in full force. They, too, walked by without even giving a glance. No one then or now was doing good by their neighbor.

I don't know about you, but I want myself and the people in my world to lead lives worthy of God's calling. I want us all to do good to our neighbor, to be sure of our direction and calling, to be good Samaritans in times of need.

As a child, one of my favorite movies was *Showboat*, with Gordon McRae. Singing at the top of his lungs, he marches toward heaven, his head high, exhorting us to not be afraid of the dark. He reminds us that we will never walk alone.

That's how it is with the Bible in our lives. With heads held high and hearts filled with hope, we march forward in confidence that the promises of God are true. "Surely I am with you always, to the very end of the age" (Matthew 28:20).

True to his word, the Lord's *Voyager* kicks in, its compasses leading the way. All the while, Captain Jesus himself walks with us every step of the way. With the captain's compass around our necks and his word in our hearts, surely we can recalculate [recalibrate] our way without a Garmin.

IN THE STORM

Take courage! It is I. Don't be afraid.

—Matthew 14:27

Texas is a conundrum when it comes to weather. One day it's hot, the next cold.

Droughts are not uncommon and recently we experienced a big one. Not as bad as the 1950s, but enough to cause concern. It ended when cold and blustery winds unexpectedly came from the north, bringing much-needed rain.

It made me think about diametrically opposed needs. While there was a definite need for rain to end the drought, I was sad that the cold wind from the north caused all the daffodils to die.

These paradoxical feelings remind me that no matter what the eye sees, God is working. Even in the storm, he's there, growing, deepening, making things bloom, preparing for the harvest. Without moisture, the long-term effects of the past nine months might have been felt in the garden for years to come. And the truth is, the sun will shine again, and the daffodils will come back next spring. They have only been stunted for a season.

I try to keep this in mind when I look around the world. The economy is floundering. The war on terror is escalating. Natural disasters, earthquakes, floods, tsunamis, tornadoes, and hurricanes all are on the rise.

Yet storms are a natural part of life, a natural part of nature. But when we are in the middle of one, it's not much fun. Just like the plants, we can't see the long-term results. We only see what is before us in that moment.

I have friends who are missionaries in Southeast Asia. Because of the severe hurricanes, earthquakes, typhoons, and tsunamis, they report that new opportunities have been opened to spread the love of Christ to people groups who have never experienced his saving grace. With each disaster, the need for compassionate hands and loving hearts trumps the need for control. Working in the worst of conditions, they do what is needed, dispense medicine, hold hands, rebuild walls, and love broken hearts. They give tirelessly to meet the physical as well as spiritual needs of those in pain.

We saw the same thing in Haiti. People filled with compassion reached out to those in pain and need. The world is full of people who are willing to give, often at great sacrifice to themselves.

A good exercise is to apply these principles to ourselves, asking how we might keep the faith when the winds blow and batter with hurricane force in our lives. How do we stay strong when everything around is falling apart? The answer is we keep our eyes focused on Jesus. We get out of the comfort of our boat if necessary.

The Gospel of Matthew teaches us a course on storm survival as we look at the disciples' response to the storm in chapter 14. Buffeted by wind and waves, they were terrified. Without Jesus, they floundered.

But when Jesus finally came to them walking on water, they refused to believe their eyes. They thought he was a ghost.

Isn't that how we are, terrified in the midst of a storm yet failing to recognize Jesus when he comes to us in its midst? Often, Jesus does just the opposite of what we expect. In this situation, the one who created the wind and waves calls Peter to step out of the boat. He tells him to walk on the water.

Sometimes our own experiences are like this. In the midst of a storm, Jesus calls us to keep our eyes focused on him, but we are too terrified to get out of the boat.

In 1996, I had an up close and personal experience with storms, boats, and disciples on a mission trip to Malawi, Central Africa. Fifty-four disciples were packed into a twenty-five-foot sailboat. We fought eight-foot waves on Lake Malawi with hope, prayer, and a small bailing bucket as our only support. Most of us later confessed that we pretty much expected to see Jesus walking across the water. It was that kind of day.

As I looked at the waves, I wondered, *If he asked me, would I get out of the boat like Peter? Surely the waves weren't this high in the story of Matthew!*

Isn't that how we are in a crisis? With limited vision, we are afraid to step out of the boat when we can't see past the next wave. But Jesus has oversight. He can see behind and before. He knows how and where he will use this experience to further his kingdom and spread the good news.

In my situation, Jesus didn't come walking across the water. He was already there, in the form of prayer warriors and intercessors who were praying for us back home. In the mystery that is prayer, they later reported that they had been awakened in the middle of the night, the exact time that we were in danger, and began to pray. That's just like God, working behind the scenes, behind every wave, in any emergency.

I have a friend who has stepped out of the boat and is walking toward Jesus in a raging storm. Called to Asia, she is moving on a wing and a prayer in order to help rehabilitate young girls who have been rescued from the slave-sex trade. Talk about high waves. Yet her eyes are fixed on Jesus as she seeks to rely on his oversight, for he knows what comes before and behind. She feels her call is to be a voice for these young girls, to raise awareness of this international problem.

Today, the economic storm rages. As savvy grandmothers, there is no better time to step out in faith. Stepping out of the boat and seeking Jesus's oversight is the best way to share the gospel with our families and friends. By walking the talk, they will learn far more from our actions and attitudes than they will from all the lectures in the world.

Recently Jim and I saw the movie *Up in the Air* with George Clooney. What a sad commentary on our time. The main character's fast-paced world had become nothing but Internet connections and upgrade perks. Relationship building and human connection were not part of his lifestyle. The movie would have served the world better if the main character had encountered a kingdom-minded believer instead of another man-eating shark who used and deceived. His transformation might have served as a beacon of hope in a world without hope. But that did not happen. Instead, the movie ended as it began, with a sense of isolation and hopelessness overriding the entire scene.

Today many of us are in the middle of that personal storm. I pray that the Lord will send his people to help open eyes to see his presence in its midst. May he give each of us courage to walk to him through the waves, for only he can see the light on the other side.

Last winter, we had the biggest snow storm since 1934 in Fort Worth. Twelve inches of powdery white turned the metroplex into a winter wonderland. Along with the beauty came downed power lines and broken branches across the city. A huge branch fell on our roof, though, by the grace of God, it did no damage. The tree doctor diagnosed this as an accident waiting to happen. Our best option was to cut the tree back and prune it to safety. What once was a canopy of shade now opened the yard to the heavenlies. Who knows what sun-loving plants will replace the previously shady garden?

In storms and trouble, we don't know what good the Lord has in store. Those in financial or other types of storms can be comforted by his presence. With eyes focused on him, may we see his plan, step out of the boat, and be a part of building his kingdom. The peach crop may be ruined and the daffodils wilted, but the growth that is generated by the living water might produce a harvest we cannot imagine or foresee

Step out of the boat…take his hand…walk through the storm. God's way is the only way to get through the wind and waves.

IN HIS WORDS

> For the word of God is living and active. Sharper than any double-edged sword, it penetrates even to dividing soul and spirit, joints and marrow; it judges the thoughts and attitudes of the heart.
>
> —Hebrews 4:12

Words are powerful things. They can build up or tear down. With just a slip of the tongue, hearts can be wounded and families destroyed. In contrast, words also have the power to heal, encourage, comfort, aid, and love. It's all in the motivation.

But words alone are not enough. The actions that follow the words are the real indicator of the heart. Here's where the rubber meets the road.

Scripture tells us to let our yes be yes and our no be no (Matthew 5:27; James 5:12). In other words, say what you mean, mean what you say. The best way to know a person is to listen to his own words.

Young children are the best at saying what they mean. Never beating around the bush, they tell it like it is. "I don't like broccoli," "My dad says you're a pushover," "I need one more piece of gum, and I promise I won't swallow it."

Recently, I attended a play at Lily's school in Austin. Since this was her first big performance, her brother James took her a dozen roses as a surprise. Dressed in her peasant's costume, just like a star on Broadway, she received them with bows and curtsies, right there on the stage.

In the middle of the play, I had a brainstorm. One of my traditions is to have my grandchildren visit one at a time—"Marme time," or "just me time," I call it, so I invited him for a visit. Usually not shy about asking to spend the night at my house, I figured he'd jump at the chance.

Kids never cease to surprise. As is the way with children, he put his head down, thought a minute, and said, "No, not today, Marme. I just want to stay home with my toys. I'm coming in a few weeks with Lily. We can spend the night then." What a great reminder to a grandmother of the consequences of broken promises. But amazingly, there was no guile or anger in him, just a yes being yes and a no being no.

I should have anticipated this response and asked him the day before, for James likes to know things ahead of time, to mull things over. He'll be a great football or soccer player someday, as he likes to mentally prepare. I had not given him enough time to prepare. Telling it like it is, James is good at words. Wouldn't it be wonderful if, as adults, we could mimic this honesty?

Jesus was good at words, too. In fact, he was the best. The disciples, as well as the Pharisees, always knew where they stood with him. Even though Jesus spent three years preparing his disciples for what was to come, they still didn't get it. They didn't believe him.

Not so with many of the politicians of our day. Often their yeses are not yes, and their nos are not no. Since their actions often don't match their words, what kind of fruit do you think they are producing? It's so easy to say what people want to hear. Without scrutiny, a wolf in sheep's clothing can easily get through the door. Looking past the words to the fruit is a good way to discern the motives of a heart.

Jesus's words and fruit are as good today as they were then. If we listen, if we watch his actions, we can gauge his character and his intent. His actions always match his words.

- "It is written… 'My house will be a house of prayer,' but you have made it 'a den of robbers'" (Luke 19:46). With that, Jesus turned over the tables and drove out those who were selling. His words and actions both demonstrated righteous anger.

- "My soul is overwhelmed with sorrow to the point of death…Stay here and keep watch" (Mark 14:34). Jesus felt sorrow so deep that his soul was agonized. With these words, he fell to the ground and sweated blood. He prayed that if possible this cup might pass from him. Sorrow so deep that falling prostrate on the ground spoke volumes.

- "I tell you the truth, today you will be with me in paradise" (Luke 23:43). Jesus's forgiveness covers a multitude of sins. With a heart so full of forgiveness and love, he reaches out to a sinner, even at the moment of death.

- "I am willing" (Matthew 8:3). With compassion, Jesus hears and heals those who come to him. He demonstrates this compassion at the humble request of a leper.

Jesus did not mince words, nor did he mince actions. You can tell a person's worth by looking at the fruit in his life. Jesus's words and actions produced much fruit.

There is a huge debate today about the exclusivity of Christ. I once heard it said that for an exclusive religion, Christianity is the most inclusive religion on earth. Never have so few given so much to so many.

Just take a look at who is first to render aid during a natural disaster. Americans are front and center with service and giving, especially Christians.

When Hurricane Katrina hit New Orleans, relief centers were set up all over Texas to house the refugees. In my hometown of Fort Worth, Camp Carter put up a number of people. Will Rogers Coliseum set up cots and a soup kitchen. Food and clothing drives were organized throughout the city. People opened their hearts and their pocketbooks, donating their talent and treasure to help those in need. I saw the devastation firsthand as I volunteered with the Red Cross. When the disaster subsided, many stayed in our area because of the love and support they'd received during this horrible time in their lives.

The January 2010 earthquake in Haiti is another example. In my own corner of the world, doctors who had contacts in Haiti through mission work loaded planes and rushed to the aid of millions, with no thought of danger to themselves.

It's not just in the Western Hemisphere that Christians give. I recently saw a special on TV showing Franklin Graham and Samaritan Purse in North Korea donating generators and dental equipment to a country in great need. A dental exchange has been organized to help prop up a sagging profession, Christianity in word and deed. Samaritan Purse was also one of the first on the ground in Haiti, with former senator Bill Frist using his time, talent, and treasure to operate on the most wounded.

Jesus is clear: there is only one way to the Father, and that's through him. Jesus's way is the only way. With the world in chaos and immorality and corruption everywhere, learning who Jesus is and what he says are the only hope for our world.

"I am the way and the truth and the life," he says. "No one comes to the Father except through me" (John 14:6).

And you can go to the bank on it.

TEACH US TO NUMBER OUR DAYS ARIGHT

> Teach us to number our days aright, that we may gain a heart of wisdom.
>
> —Psalm 90:12

It is appointed unto man a time to live and a time to die, for the Lord has numbered our days. He knows every hair on our head, every bone in our body. He cherishes every wrinkle on our face, every joint and marrow.

Yes, the Lord is in charge.

As the years fly by and I move forward in the journey, I am more aware that it's my days that are numbered. Time is growing short. Numbering my days and applying my heart to wisdom are two things I want to do in the time I have left on this earth.

Lucky for me, numbering my days is not in my hands. That's totally up to God. Only he knows what time is appointed for me. I can eat right, exercise, watch my weight, and live a healthy lifestyle, but God is the perfector of my time.

Recently, a friend who was seventy-two died. Thin, in great health, he didn't smoke or drink and exercised regularly. With no warning, he had a massive heart attack while serving a tie-breaker on the tennis courts. Though he did all the right things, he had no control over his destiny. You just never know when your number will be called.

We can do the best we can with our bodies, but gaining a heart of wisdom is another matter. Listening to the Lord, making note of the opportunities placed before us, is the best way I know of gaining a heart of wisdom.

Wisdom is a difficult concept to grasp. I suspect it was for Solomon, too, when he first began. But as Christians, we have a teacher and guide who brings us into all knowledge and truth. The Holy Spirit brings wisdom down to our size in a language we can understand.

There are many different languages in the world, and we all hear in our language of choice. James has been learning Spanish in school. While staying at his house, I noticed he repeatedly asked me the names of the colors of the rainbow in Spanish.

It took me a while to figure out that he was having trouble remembering the words. Reverting back to my tried and true Grandmother favorite, the ice cream store, I took him out for a hot fudge sundae. He loves ice cream, and I can't think of a better way to get my juices flowing than with chocolate on board. My brainstorm allowed me to kill two birds with one stone.

As previously mentioned, James learns by playing games. Remember Chicken Foot, Sorry, and Monopoly? I figured this was the perfect opportunity to bring in the game card.

I started with associations: "Yellow is *Amarillo.* You can remember because both words have "yo" at the end. Red is *rojo.* The r sound in both words is like a barking dog—*rrr.*

It didn't take long for him to get the idea. *Verde,* green, became tree, bark, and grass. Don't ask me about that connection; it's over my head, but in his mind, it made sense.

As follow up, I gave him a Spanish dictionary with pictures for a learning tool. I'm told he consults it often. If history is any indicator, he will master Spanish, just as he did Chicken Foot, Sorry, and Monopoly.

I'd like to think that this experience overflowed from a heart of wisdom. After all, God teaches us to number our days aright when we're open and ready. If we listen carefully and look for Holy Spirit moments, we might hear his call. That's what I'm working on.

Numbering my days aright has been moved to the top of my to-do list. I want to be a woman of wisdom, a godly guide and mentor with biblical principles ordering my thinking. I desire that the Living Word would speak through me in everything I do and every person I meet. It all has to do with listening and divine opportunities.

I want to be available and present, so that I will not miss any opportunity to share the wisdom that has been handed down from the Father through his Holy Spirit to me.

Hodge loves music and has since the moment of his birth. Even before he could talk, he had perfect pitch. As a baby, he made humming sounds when the electric gate opener or the lawn mower was going off in the neighborhood. Even an airplane flying overhead brought a symphonic chord.

I'm slow, but eventually I surmised that he was copying each sound with perfect pitch. I figured, if James learns by games and Lily learns by storytelling, perhaps Hodge learns by music. I tried an experiment, which I've been perfecting ever since.

I started with simple songs and ditties that I thought he'd like. Now we have moved into more complex rhymes. He initiates the theme, and I make up the song. I'm starting to weave simple, educational information into the rhythm. I'm hoping that my song-writing skills will grow in proportion to his aging. My goal is to weave life lessons into future songs. We'll see. A Bette Midler I'm not. Anyone listening would not be impressed. It's just Marme music, but for Hodge and me, it's our special time.

Holy Spirit moments come in all shapes and sizes. Sometimes they come in a conversation, a dream, a knowing, a discomfort, or a heart quickening. Recognizing these moments can make a difference in our lives and in the lives of others as well. Only by being in constant contact with the Spirit can we recognize and speak wisdom into others when they manifest in our world.

When Lily's rabbit, Cookie, died, she was very concerned about where he had gone. Was he dead? Was he in heaven? She continued to ask for reassurance that yes, he was in heaven with Granddad and Grandmother Norman. And yes, our beloved dog, Abbey, was there also. A long conversation ensued on the telephone about what they were doing at that very moment, with both of our imaginations running wild. Of course, Jesus was at the center of that conversation. Unexpectedly, without prompting, she confided that she was glad Cookie was in heaven with Abbey; she was glad that Jesus was there and that she had Jesus in her heart.

Sometimes Holy Spirit moments come out of the clear blue. Once during a lunch at Chick-fil-A, James piped up to say, "Guess who my favorite person is?"

I went through every sports star I could think of but to no avail.

Finally he asked, "Do you give?"

"I do," I replied.

"It starts with a G, and it's God. You know why? Because God created me, and Jesus saved me." Now who could have predicted that exchange?

Often Holy Spirit moments come in the car in the form of a tiny voice from the backseat. One Sunday after taking Strother to church, he asked why I talked to God. I told him it was because I had a lot of things on my mind, and I knew that God was my friend and would help me take care of them.

Then he asked if I talk to God about him. I responded with a resounding yes, stressing how grateful I am that God created him so special and brought him into my life.

I have no idea what precipitated this discussion. But he seemed pleased with the exchange, and I was elated with the Holy Spirit opening.

Sometimes the Holy Spirit moves in unexpected ways as an unexpected gift. Recently I attended a luncheon with pastors from all over the city. At the end, a man I had been in a jail ministry with years before walked across the room to speak to me. He put a piece of a puzzle in place for me regarding my own ministry.

For years the Lord had placed on my heart to learn Spanish. Frustrated by being unable to find teaching material that spoke the language of the Bible, I had given up. There in the middle of the banquet hall, this man guided me through his English/Spanish Bible, encouraging me as he pointed out specific words for ministry. Now I have my own English/Spanish bible. The going is slow, but I'm ready and moving forward.

We've all had these moments. They are different for each of us. What is important is that we listen to the promptings of the Holy Spirit and act upon them using the wisdom and guidance he gives. When we feel a nudge in a certain direction, taking an action can make a difference, sometimes for eternity.

One day I had a nudge on the way to my exercise class. Always late, I rushed in at the last minute, brushing past a woman at the door in a flurry. As I opened the door to the class, I was prompted by the Holy Spirit to go back and talk to her. What ensued was a lengthy conversation with a woman who had just found out she had cancer and was having a really bad day. Helpless, alone, she needed a comforting word from the Lord. How grateful I am that he chose me that day, to pour out the soothing words of salvation to her soul, a healing balm that no cancer drug can match.

I wish I had been more in tune with the Spirit when I was younger. I wasn't. No telling how many opportunities I missed.

But the good news is that I am in tune today. I can't cry over spilt milk. I must begin now, for this is the day that the Lord has made. This is the day for this savvy grandmother to number my days aright and let the Lord teach me how to have a heart of wisdom. This is an appointment I don't want to miss.

I PRAY YOU ENOUGH

> I pray that you may be active in sharing your faith, so that you will have a full understanding of every good thing we have in Christ.
>
> —Philemon 1:6

Recently, a friend sent me an e-mail that told the story of a mother and daughter who were saying good-bye at the airport. As they embraced, the mother said, "I love you, and I pray you enough." Puzzled, the one who overheard questioned the mother. She explained that "praying you enough" was a prayer her family had prayed for one another over the generations.

I have been reflecting on this prayer and what praying one enough means in my life.

I'm reminded of the founding fathers, who gave their all for future generations and freedom in Christ. They certainly prayed us enough. I remember the words and rights they set down in the Declaration of Independence and Constitution. But most of all, I'm reminded of the God who made it all possible. So it's not implausible to stop and give glory to God for our many blessings. As we celebrate these amazing freedoms, it's important to remember the men and women, past and present who have made all of this possible.

I'm convinced that the founding fathers were endowed with great wisdom by our Creator. Their days had certainly been numbered aright. The decisions they made, the sacrifices they suffered, sharpened their iron will. Without the anointing of God, they would surely have failed.

Today we need more founding fathers and mothers with wills of steel, well-educated students of history, and faith-filled disciples—people who are sold out to God and willing to take a stand for Christ. We need more witnesses who are willing to give verbal testimony to the power of God as he reveals himself in lives, sharing truth, wherever it resides, often touching the deepest places of the heart. People just know when something is authentic and true.

I know with every fiber of my being that the Bible is true. Words passed down from mouth to papyrus scrolls, it touches minds and hearts with the presence of the living God. The Scripture tells us that the Word of God is living and active, stronger than any two-edged sword that pierces to the core of joint and marrow (Hebrews 4:12).

Think about a double-edged sword. Shiny and sharp, it cuts a sliver of paper with the flick of a wrist. It judges the thoughts and attitudes of the heart. Jesus is the Word made flesh, that double-edged sword that cuts to the heart of every human on earth. One day every person will be called before him to give an accounting of his life. How blessed we are to know him as Lord and Savior. Because his Spirit resides in those who believe, we are privileged to be his representatives, his ambassadors, here on earth.

The older I get, the more convinced I am that being an ambassador involves giving a witness or a testimony. In fact, the truth is the most powerful sword we have in our arsenal.

A wise woman once told me that the Scriptures tell us to be ready in and out of season. In other words, be prepared to give an answer to the hope that is within you (1 Peter 3:15). I believe that the best way to share this hope is to prepare three testimonies, short, powerful stories of coming to faith: the first, only thirty seconds to be used for a quick encounter; the second, two to three minutes for those who ask; and the third, twenty to thirty minutes for larger groups. That way we will be prepared in and out of season.

An experience I had attests to the truth of this exercise. As a friend and I rode the ski lift up Grand Butte Mountain in Colorado, a conversation turned to things of the heart. After she shared an issue in her life, she suddenly stopped and said, "I know you are a spiritual person. Tell me," she asked, "why do you believe in God?"

I was taken aback; the question was totally unexpected, and I was not prepared. I knew that the end of the lift was two to three minutes away. There was not enough time to tell my story. I mumbled something simple and inane and let the moment pass.

That moment never came again. I've often wondered what the sword of Christ could have effected had I been prepared.

Today the world needs more double-edged swords, men and women of steel and faith, savvy grandparents who are unafraid and immovable. The world cries out for George Washington and Thomas Jefferson, for grandparents who are active, involved, and bold, willing to take a stand for Christ. With our country and history in danger, where are the grandmothers who will take a stand for freedom and pass on the great traditions of this country and the Christian faith to the next generation?

As swords, we may not be as shiny or sharp as we used to be, but our best tools are still our heads and hearts. By studying history, learning the Bible, memorizing and applying truth, we can penetrate the souls of families and friends to joint and marrow. Our creed is to know the truth, and the truth shall set us free (John 8:32).

As savvy grandmothers, our mantra is to stand up, stand up for Jesus. Shout it from the rooftops. Pray for our children, grandchildren, friends, neighbors, and coworkers, that they may enjoy the rich traditions and heritage that we have been privileged to enjoy.

So I pray you enough courage to stand strong, be bold, and speak in public what the Lord gives in private. Whether a salvation testimony or a powerful spiritual experience, the truth is never lost. It penetrates the highest wall, the deepest valley.

I know. I learned my lesson well. After returning from a mission trip to Belize in 2007, I was again instructed to prepare the same three testimonies just in case. This time I was obedient. No one could have predicted the powerful conversations that came about as a result of my sharing my experience with God as he worked in and among his people in Belize.

Part of my testimony involved a word the Lord gave me as my plane landed in Belize City. "Look out the window," my heart prompted.

As I obeyed, I saw a sea of green. Low green bushes and shrubs surrounded the runway. But every so often there were tall trees, their trunks and canopies standing high above the fray, tall, straight, reaching to the heavens.

Again my heart spoke, "Look for the tall trees. There are believers here. You will know them because they stand high and above the rest." And they did.

Since then, my prayer has been that we, like those tall trees, will stand tall and strong, high and above the rest.

Like the Statue of Liberty, who stands at the entrance of New York Harbor, may we stand at the door of Christ. She holds a book and a torch; we hold the Bible and the light of Christ.

Her words are: "Give me your tired, your poor, your huddled masses yearning to breathe free…The wretched refuse of your teeming shore…Send these, the homeless, tempest-tossed to me…I lift my lamp beside the golden door."[1]

Our words are Christ's words: "Come unto me, all you who are weary and burdened, and I will give you rest" (Matthew 11:28). "God so loved the world, that he gave his one and only Son, that whoever believes in him shall not perish but have eternal life" (John 3:16). "Here is a trustworthy saying that deserves full acceptance: Christ Jesus came into the world to save sinners" (1Timothy 1:15).

As women of faith, we have the opportunity to stand tall at the entrance of hearts. Pray that these hearts may rejoice in the rich traditions and heritage that we have been privileged to enjoy. Holding the Bible and the light of Christ, we hold a gift that must be passed on.

So, as we end our reflections and board the plane for the next phase of our journey, we prepare our swan song for the world. May our suitcases be filled with wonder and our hearts with the Word of God. May we be sharp as a double-edged sword and bold in sharing testimonies of faith. May we be steeled by the will of Christ and accompanied by the sword of the Spirit.

My prayer is that we will all pray enough as we stand tall and strong against the evil one. Be bold in your witness, use your time, talent and treasure wisely, build up the kingdom of heaven, always look toward the Captain, and pass on the faith that has been passed on to you.

So all aboard! Let the voyage begin.

FROM A GRANDCHILD'S PERSPECTIVE

From 1945 to 1960 one of the most popular radio and TV shows of the day was called "House Party." Hosted by Art Linkletter, this variety show is best remembered for the appropriately named segment "Kids Say the Darndest Things." His interviews with children from five to ten-years-old were legendary. Over his twenty-three-year career, Linkletter interviewed approximately 23,000 children. This popular segment later led to a TV series by the same name from January 1998 to June 2000, hosted by Bill Cosby. I'm no Art Linkletter or Bill Cosby, but I do a pretty good imitation. And I'd put my grandkids up against those kids any day.

Following are the five Norman grandkids' responses to questions regarding life, grandparents, wisdom, and God.

Jack – Age 12

1. Who are grandparents, and what do you like to do with them?

   "Grandparents are always there to help you out and care for you. Like when parents aren't there. I love to do go-carts, play golf, go to the ranch and work the cattle, play tennis and golf with grandparents. I like to ride in the pickup with Big Dad. He is really funny because he yells,

"Yeehaw" at the top of his lungs. Marme is funny because she always wants to buy stuff for us."

2. What is wisdom, and do you think grandparents have it?

"Wisdom is knowledge. A person has it when they are clever in an area or are an old-timer. Like a book I read about a man in Alaska. The main character did not listen to the old-timer who had wisdom, and he died because of it. I think grandparents have a lot of wisdom. Parents don't have as much as grandparents because they haven't lived as long."

3. What do you like about working cattle at the ranch, and why?

"I love working cattle at the ranch 'cause I like being with the family. I like hard work, and I appreciate how Big Dad has us every year and pays me."

4. You used to have long hair. Why did you decide to cut it?

"I don't know. I liked long hair when I had it, but it got in my way and bugged me. I couldn't see very well, so I cut it. Besides, I'm at a new school, and there's not as much long hair there."

5. What did you learn about the history of our country when you visited Washington D.C.?

"I learned a lot about our country. I definitely liked the Capitol and the White House, and I loved walking through them and looking at stuff. If I had to pick my favorite thing it would be seeing the White House. I like knowing where the president is speaking from when he's on TV because I've seen it. I learned a lot in Washington. I learned that the Founding Fathers did a good job. George Washington was really brave to do what he did for our country. He believed in what he said and then he did it."

6. What is critical thinking, and do you think you have it when you make decisions?

"Critical thinking is when you're in a tough spot and you can think fast and quickly in a sticky situation. I think I use critical thinking, and I think I make pretty good decisions. Last year I saved my money from Big Dad and mowed yards and added birthday money and bought a computer. That was a pretty good decision."

7. Who is God and what is faith?

"Faith is like following something. My faith in God is that I go to chapel every morning for thirty minutes. I like the different songs and stuff. And I like the connection you have to God in church. I pray, and I think I follow God pretty well. He will listen to you and forgive your sins, but you need to be faithful not to say his name in vain."

8. Who is Jesus?

"Jesus is Christ the Savior. I'm taking theology, and I'm learning all about Christianity and all religions. It's pretty cool."

Lily – Age 10

1. What are grandparents, and what do you like to do with them?

"Grandparents are old, but they're really nice. And they aren't scary a bit. My grandparents aren't old. They take me to Chuck E. Cheese. They also bake cookies with me. They take me to the park with Daisy and play Sorry and Chicken Foot. I like to play because I win a lot."

2. When you were younger, you used to play Dora and Webkinz on the Internet. Was that fun?

"I don't like Dora and Webkinz anymore—that's for kids. But I like the Internet. I like to use my iPod. I get to watch cat videos on YouTube, and they're very funny."

3. You are a great storyteller and listener. Describe a story that you and Marme tell that you really like.

"One story I like is about dragons. It's about a boy named Sir William whose dad was king. He went out to hunt dragons so he could become a man. He was afraid to go, but he went anyway. Sir William was gone a month and never saw a dragon. But he crossed a river, slept in a cave, and made it through a snow storm without a parka. Later his dad told him that dragons were not real. Dragons were in his own mind. By crossing the river, sleeping in the cave and the snow storm, he killed the dragons in his mind. I like the story 'cause now he could be a man."

4. What to you like about the ranch and why?

"I like the ranch because you have to take care of and feed the cows. If you don't, they will die. Then they'll go to heaven and be with God. I also like horses because they are fun and run very fast. I am taking horseback riding lessons in Austin. My favorite horse is Nikki at my lessons and Lucky at the ranch."

5. Now that you are a tween, how do you like your new bedroom?

"I like it—especially all the pink and orange. They're my favorite colors. My pink kitty looks really cute on my new bedspread, and I love my new polka-dot chair."

6. Who is God?

"God lives in heaven, and he loves us. Abbey and Jakers and Cookie and the dead cows are all in heaven with him."

Who is Jesus?

"Jesus died on the cross for us."

James – Age 7

1. What are grandparents, and what do you like to do with them?

   "Grandparents are nice. And they're easy to have fun with. Some grandparents are old 'cause they don't run, and they say weird stuff. My grandparents are fun, and I like to do lots of stuff with them, like play golf, baseball, swing, play games."

2. How are you doing in Spanish and why?

   "I'm still not so good at Spanish. I sort of like it. I learn a lot from my Spanish teacher at school. I've already memorized all the colors, and I can count to thirty-nine."

3. How are you at playing games, and why do you like them?

   "I'm a really good game player. I love Monopoly and Sorry—they're my favorite 'cause I always win. I'm so good at games because I play 'em a lot."

4. You like to wear football jerseys. Why?

   "Football jerseys don't make you hot. I love sports and watch 'em on TV whenever I can. My favorite football team is the Cowboys 'cause they're in my state. I also like baseball. The Rangers are my favorite baseball team. Then the Yankess, and then the Fort Worth Cats. I've tried to catch a baseball with my glove when I go to a game, but I can't 'cause they never hit it to me."

5. What do you like about praying?

   "It's good to pray. Sometimes I get on my knees and put my hands together and say whatever I want to say to God. That's called praying."

6. Who is God?

   "God is someone who makes people. He's nice and he powers the world."

7. Who is Jesus?

"He's dead. Someone killed him. I know a story about him though. We never learn about him in school—they don't teach about him there. Only at church. But I don't like church much."

Strother – Age 5

1. What are grandparents, and what do you like to do with them?

"Grandparents are fun, and they have wrinkles. My Marme has wrinkles on her neck 'cause she's old. Big Dad has wrinkles on his hand. That's 'cause he has wisdom. I don't have wrinkles. My teacher has wrinkles on her hand. But she doesn't have wisdom. I do a lot with grandparents, like watch TV, build Legos, ride bicycles, swim, and have picnics. I really like the Bungee at the mall, LegoLand, and church. I like Tic Tac Toe 'cause I always win. I'm good at it 'cause I'm so tall for my age."

2. Why do you like church?

"I like Sunday school 'cause we wave palm trees. I also like the songs. I want to have 'community' (*communion*) with church. Once we learned about a man who saw a burning bush. I remembered him 'cause Marme told me how people put him in a basket and sent him into a lake. He also talked to God in a bush."

3. Once you put a straw in your ear and walked down the stairs. Why did you do that?

"I don't remember. But I don't think it would hurt. I think I'd rather put a straw in my nose. That wouldn't hurt either. I have a tough nose."

4. When you were two years old, you jumped off the high diving board. Do you remember why you did this?

"I don't remember, but I wasn't scared. You know why? 'Cause I kept my eyes closed. My papa was in the water to catch me. And my papa can do anything."

5. Who is God?

    "God lives in heaven. He lives in the clouds, but he can't see through the clouds. It's a mystery how he sees me. God made the sun and everything. He even made you and me and Hodge. See, God made the sun for us today so we could play. The sun makes things grow. God makes me grow. I growed so much I weigh forty pounds."

6. Who is Jesus?

    Jesus is God's son

Hodge – Age 2 ½

1. What are grandparents, and what do you like to do with them?

    "Marme, Big Dad, Nana. Look at booboos. I have one, two, three, four booboos. I like Dora, sing, tennis, basket, baseballs, 'Tar Wars' (*Star Wars)*, knock knock (*knock knock jokes*), Trick You. I like Hiding (Hide and Seek) and I swing. NEVER EVER stand up in swing. I like gum and breakfast. I eat Big Dad's cereal. No cereal at my house. Only Big Dad's house."

2. What do you like to say a lot to Marme and Big Dad, and what are your favorite songs?

    "'I dood it.' I sing 'Row Da Boat,' 'McDonald's Farm,' 'Da Boat Went Over Da Moutain,' 'Off We Go (about Tar Wars)." I sing twinkle, twinkle, little tar (star)…wonder what you are." I sing ABCD in my (water) glass.

3. What do you like to eat at Marme and Big Dad's house?

    "Gum and treats. I sit with Strudder and watch TV. I eat gold fish. I eat gum."

(Immediately following question))

"Big Dad, you got gum?"

"No, I don't have gum."

"Aw, man!"

4. Why do you like church?

   "Sing Jesus Loves and leaves (*Palms*). Amen."

5. Who is God?

   "The sun."

6. Who is Jesus?

   "Jesus loves."

STUDY QUESTIONS AND PERSONAL REFLECTION

Below are study questions by chapter, good for individual meditation or group reflection.

Part 1: Revisiting the Season of Fall

1. What collections or personal reminders keep your personal history in the forefront? How are you evaluating your life? What kingdom values, principles, promises, hopes, or dreams do you want to incorporate into the rest of your life?

2. As a savvy grandmother, what verses do you want to recite for the King? What are two stories of faith you would like to leave as a legacy, and how will you do it?

3. Name three women in your life who mentored or influenced you. What difference did they make in your life?

4. What areas in your life do you need to remodel, redecorate, revamp, or redo? How will these changes help make you a savvy grandmother?

5. Write your own cardboard testimony and practice it as a short testimony should anyone ask.

6. What actions in your life do you need to check with Scripture to make sure you are not creating a fog in the lives of those around you?

Part 2: Revisiting the Legacy

7. In your suitcase on wheels, which pile of emotional baggage—unresolved issues, bitter roots, unresolved grief, lost dreams and expectations or the discard pile—do you need to deal with first and why? How will you go about it?

8. Name two parachute packers in your life and why they are important. Now name two people for whom you are a parachute packer and why.

9. What would you like on your tombstone? How do these words reflect your life?

10. Think of a time when you got off God's path. What did the Lord do to get your attention? Did you return to his path or go your own way?

11. Think of a time when your spiritual temperature was all over the map. How did the Lord put his spiritual thermometer before you?

12. Think of three times recently you prayed aloud with a family member or friend. If not, why not, and what would it take for you to step out in faith and do so?

Part 3: Revisiting Nursery Rhymes and Fairy Tales

13. Think of a weak link in your life when a strong wind was able to blow your door down. What did you do to rehinge yourself to the Father, Son, and Holy Spirit?

14. How are you mentoring women or helping grandchildren or young people in the decision-making process?

15. Describe an example, either in your family or society, where you are you concerned about the end justifying the means. What do you plan to do about it?

16. Name a time in your life when as one of the King's men, you brought the wounded and broken to the throne of God.

17. Where in your life have you been rebellious and jumped over a candlestick?

18. How and what are you doing in the community to model Christian values? Think of a specific example where you made a difference.

Part 4: Revisiting Holidays and Church Traditions

19. Think of three ways you are being a servant and washing dirty feet in the community. If you don't have any examples, what will you do today to begin serving your community?

20. Where do you go for iron to sharpen your iron? Where are you in God's army right now? Are you on the narrow path, taking a shortcut, bogged down, dragging others along, or just sitting and waiting for orders?

21. Are you on the world's merry-go-round or on God's carousel? What would it take to get off the merry-go-round and declare that Jesus is Lord to the world?

22. Describe a time you shared the gospel that brought light into a dark life.

23. What new way will you impart the depth of Mary and Joseph's faith to a secular world during Advent and Christmas?

24. What is your "savvy grandmother" plan to get Christ back into Christmas?

Part 5: Revisiting History

25. Do you know the Judeo-Christian principles that are the foundation of our country? If not, research and share two you read in this chapter that surprised you.

26. In what ways are you using your gifts and talents to pass on history to the next generation? If not, how will you begin?

27. What freedom in our country do you most cherish? Do you know who fought and died to make that freedom a reality? How far would you go to maintain that freedom for the next generation?

28. What are your gifts and talents? How will you use them for the kingdom in the rest of your life?

29. What time period in history interests you the most? How will you research and pass on this truth to the next generation?

30. What generational healing has been passed down in your family? What generational sin needs to be healed?

Part 6: Revisiting Spiritual Truth

31. What seeds, byproducts, or successes are you setting aside from last year's harvest as your first fruits? How will you offer them to God?

32. What area of your life needs to be recalculated? [recalibrated?] What biblical principles act as the moral compass to help you find your way?

33. Think of a storm in your life when Jesus came walking on the water. Did you get out of the boat? If not, why not?

34. Think of a person in your life whose actions do not match his or her words. Now think of someone whose words and actions match. What can you learn from these two people?

35. What has the Holy Spirit recently prompted you to do? Have you been obedient and if not, why not? What can you do to remedy that?

36. Think of a symbol or metaphor, like the Statue of Liberty, that expresses your desire to stand fast and be a double-edged sword. What changes do you need to make in order to accomplish this goal?

Part 7: From A Grandchild's Perspective

37. What would your grandchild, friends, and neighbors say about your role in their lives?

38. How have you impacted your environment, specifically your grandchild, for Christ?

ENDNOTES

Introduction: A Savvy Grandmother's Legacy

1. Marty Norman, *Generation G* (Nashville: Thomas Nelson, 2007).

Chapter 2: My Heart Is Stirred

1. "Just You Wait," *My Fair Lady: A Musical Play in Two Acts*. Based on *Pygmalion* by George Bernard Shaw. Adaptation and lyrics by Alan Jay Lerner, Music by Frederick Loewe (New York: Doward-McCann, Inc., 1956).

Chapter 3: The Power of Influence

1. United States Department of Commerce, Economic and Statistics Administration, U.S. Census Bureau, the Official Statistics, 1997, http://www.census,gov/Press-release.

Chapter 5: Silver Hair, Silver Threads

1. Heather Barbieri, *The Lacemakers of Glenamare* (New York: Harper, 2009), epigraph.

Chapter 9: Two Angels and a Stone

1. Greg Mortenson, *Stones into Schools: Promoting Peace with Books, Not Bombs, in Afghanistan and Pakistan* (New York: Viking, 2009), page 98.

2. "Thank You," words and music by Ray Boltz, copyright 1988 Gather Music/ASCAP.

Chapter 6: If There's a Mistake in the Pulpit, There Will Be a Fog in the Pews

1. *Webster's Collegiate Dictionary*, 11th ed. (New York: Merriam-Webster, 2005), s.v. "pastor."

2. Ibid., s.v. "fog."

Chapter 13: The Three Little Pigs

1. David Sessions, "Brit Hume: Tiger Woods Should 'Turn to the Christian Faith,'" Politics Daily, 4 January 2010.

Chapter 19: Dirty Feet

1. The Book of Common Prayer, Rite II, 362.

Chapter 21: Who Do You Say I Am?

1. For information on how you can purchase these Christian-themed Easter eggs from FamilyLife, called "Resurrection Eggs," see http://www.shopfamilylife.com/resurrection-eggs.html.

Chapter 23: What Is Conceived in Her

1. *Webster's Collegiate Dictionary*, 11th ed. (New York: Merriam-Webster, 2005), s.v. "handmaiden."

2. Ibid., s.v. "advent."

Chapter 25: We Hold These Truths to Be Self-Evident

1. Robert Lincoln, *Lives of the Presidents of the United States, with Biographical Notices of the Signers of the Declaration of Independence* (Brattleboro Typographical Company, 1839); John and Katherine Bakeless, *Signers of the Declaration* (Boston: Houghton Mifflin, 1969); *Biographical Directory of the United States Congress, 1774–1989* (Washington, D.C.; U.S. Government Printing Office, 1989). As quoted on Celebratelove.com.

2. Good News Daily, 14 October 2006; www.goodnewsdaily.net.

3. U.S. Const., preamble

4. *World Book Encyclopedia,* Vol. 5 (Chicago: World Book Inc., 1979), 68; s.v. "Declaration of Independence."

5. Wendy J. Saxton, *The Jonah Chronicles* (Enumclaw, WA: Pleasant Word/Winepress, 2009).

Chapter 26: The Times Are A' Changin

1. *Webster's Collegiate Dictionary*, 11th ed. (New York: Merriam-Webster, 2005), s.v. "revolution."

2. Sally Clarkson, *The Mission of Motherhood: Touching Your Child's Heart for Eternity* (Colorado Springs: WaterBrook, 2003).

Chapter 28: Ten Seniors Whose Faith Changed the World

1. NIV *Life Application Study Bible,* June 1978 (Revised August 1983).

2. Corrie Ten Boom with Elizabeth and John Sherrill, *The Hiding Place* (New York: Hendrickson, 2009).

3. David Wilkerson and John Sherrill, *The Cross and the Switchblade*, 45th ann. ed. (Ada, MI: Chosen, 2008).

4. Chapter 29: The Eagle Has Landed

5. Dr. David R. Williams, "The Apollo 8 Christmas Eve Broadcast," 28 September 2007; dave.williams@nasa.gov. Accessed 4 June 2010.

6. U.S. Const., First Amendment

7. Buzz Aldrin, *Magnificent Desolation: The Long Journey Home from the Moon* (New York: Harmony, 2009).

8. Neil Armstrong, "Upon Landing on the Moon—July 20, 1969," www.quotationspage.com. Accessed 4 June 2010.

Chapter 30: Do the Right Thing

1. Mike Hukabee, *Do the Right Thing: Inside the Movement That's Bringing Common Sense Back to America* (New York: Sentinel Trade, 2009).

2. Abraham Lincoln, Gettysburg Address, 19 November 1863, available at http://showcase.netins.net/web/creative/lincoln/speeches/gettysburg.htm. Accessed 21 April 2010.

Chapter 36: I Pray You Enough

1. Emma Lazarus, "The New Colossus," available at http://www.statueliberty.net/statue-of-liberty-poem.html. Accessed 21 April 2010.